ECO-INTERIORS

ECO-INTERIORS

A GUIDE TO
ENVIRONMENTALLY CONSCIOUS INTERIOR DESIGN

Grazyna Pilatowicz

John Wiley & Sons, Inc.
New York • Chichester • Brisbane • Toronto • Singapore

Library of Congress Cataloging in Publication Data:

Pilatowicz, Grazyna, 1954–
    Eco-interiors : guide to environmentally conscious interior design
  / by Grazyna Pilatowicz.
        p.   cm.
    Includes bibliographical references
    ISBN 0-471-04045-2 (pbk.)
    1. Interior decoration—Environmental aspects.   I. Title.
NK2113. P55 1994   94-30570
729—dc20

Dedicated to my husband,
Howard Stern.
For your participation in gathering
information and illustrative materials;
for your architectural expertise; for your
help in understanding issues involved
and in forming thoughts into the words; for
your encouragement, understanding
and patience–I thank you.

Preface

"What is the use of a house
if you don't have a decent planet to put it on?"
Henry David Thoreau

The objective of this book is to bring together the most important information on environmentally conscious interior design, and to present it in a comprehensive, convenient, reader-friendly form. Through this initial step I hope to awaken sensitivity among interior designers and interior design students, provide the most needed basic body of knowledge and encourage further interest and application of the theory into practice. Because environmental research is a constantly developing discipline, *Eco-Interiors* points out available sources of information rather than supplying today's answers, which may change tomorrow. It is important that this book be viewed as an introduction for responsible designers who are seeking information, and that the information provided be continuously updated with each designer's personal research.

The introduction to *Eco-Interiors* describes the philosophy of the book, focusing on the social responsibilities and professional ethics of interior designers. Part I, Environmental Issues, characterizes global and indoor environmental concerns. This is the realm that interior designers influence through their practice and the critical choices they make every day. Part II, Interior Design Process, focuses on the specific problems designers face while designing indoor spaces, specifying furniture, equipment and materials. In Part III, readers will find descriptions of projects – Case Studies – that in various degrees address environmental concerns. Most of the projects discussed had follow-up studies devoted either to energy efficiency or to indoor air quality. The three Parts are divided into chapters, and most chapters end with a subject specific bibliography. In addition, Part IV, Existing Resources, lists related legislation and certification initiatives, organizations, publications and literature. At the back of the book, the reader will find a list of abbreviations and a bibliography.

For additional ease each part of the book is coded with an identifying icon:

General
Statements

Environmental
Issues

Interior Design
Process

Case Studies

Existing
Resources

No product advertisement is intended. The examples are used solely for explanatory purposes and should be treated as such.

• • •

No research can be done in solitude. I am grateful to all of those who were helpful during the process of working on this manuscript: to Julius Panero for his initial encouragement; to Larry Israel for many valuable suggestions; to Martin Zelnik for persistent gathering of information; to Ron Lubman for showing me the way to make the computer work for me; all of them are members of the Fashion Institute of Technology in New York Interior Design faculty.

My appreciation goes also to Asher Derman for highly professional comments and generosity in sharing knowledge as illustrated by his direct input into this publication.

I am the most grateful to Al Rios for struggling through the text, providing constructive criticisms and superbly professional editing.

You all have been the most helpful.

Contents

"To understand the meaning of the word ecosystem and to appreciate the role that this word plays in communicating man's increasing concern about his environment, one should consider the holistic concept that underlies the term. Holism, in this connotation, is based on the theory that living components (organisms, including man) and nonliving components (the physical environment) function together as a whole according to well-defined physical and biological laws. Also fundamental to this concept is a generalization known as the theory of integrative levels or the theory of hierarchical controls. By this is meant that as components are added to create larger functional units, additional attributes come into focus, attributes not present or not evident from the behavior of the separate components."

Ecosystems, 1992 Britannica Book of the Year.

Introduction

The quality of the environment, both natural and man-made, has unlimited influence on peoples' behavior and their physical and psychological well-being. Some effects of that influence are immediately noticeable; others happen in more subtle ways.

Interior designers shape the indoor environment in which people live, work, perform day-to-day tasks and rest. In doing so, interior designers influence how people think, feel, and function. It is appropriate to say that, through shaping the spaces, designers shape the patterns of peoples' behavior. Since designers affect a society's sensitivity and thinking, the aesthetics and ethics of the designs must respond to the most burning issues of the contemporary world. This awareness is especially important now, at this critical time in the life of our planet, when humanity is facing twin catastrophes: natural resources depletion and environmental degradation. "We have taken clean air and pure water for granted for the first ten million years or so, but now this picture has changed drastically. While the reasons for our poisoned air and polluted streams and lakes are fairly complex, it must be admitted that the designers and design industry in general, are certainly co-responsible with others for this appalling state of affairs" (Papanek, p.46).

Accelerating world population, paralleled by the scientific and technological revolution, completely transformed our relationship with the environment. Never before in the history of humankind have we

had the power to change the Earth's climate and to harm our own ecosystem, passing the point of no return. The threat of global destruction, comparable only with nuclear disaster, was never so close. "Global warming, ozone depletion, the loss of living species, deforestation–they all have a common cause: the new relationship between human civilization and the earth's natural balance" (Gore, p.31).

The list of destructive human impacts on the biosphere is endless. As in any microcosm, many environmental issues can be found in the relatively small field of interior design: the devastating methods of generating energy, polluting industries, species being endangered, problems with solid waste, destruction of forests, all come to focus. The basic elements – air, water and earth – are all affected by the decisions designers make every day.

Global environment and indoor environment are interdependent and, while striving to achieve an "environmentally conscious interior," it is necessary to take into consideration the influence on both outside and inside environment. The impact on the global environment is a result of the materials and methods for construction and finishing that are specified, and of the future energy consumption that the design will require, as well as of the future waste and pollution generated by the interior. An additional set of criteria has to be considered in order to provide occupants with "healthy interiors" including: clean indoor air, suitable thermal and acoustic conditions, functional and aesthetically pleasing spaces, appropriately resolved lighting, colors and textures. Luckily, in most circumstances, the outdoor and the indoor criteria are compatible and it is possible to have materials and methods which are good for both the global environment and healthy interiors.

It is not easy to be "a conscious designer." The problem starts as soon as the complexity of the issues is realized. Reading published literature does not always help, since too often the reader faces the dilemma of contradicting opinions. Lacking access to the research processes makes it very difficult, if not impossible, to make knowledgeable decisions. The feeling of confusion is increased by the questionable quality of some information, which itself becomes a form of pollution. Sometimes it is necessary to recognize that opinions on various environmental issues are influenced by the interests of the writer or the industry he/she represents.

It is also important to realize that sometimes there is no perfect solution, and we can only choose the one that is less damaging to the environment.

The problems grow even more complex when studying the global scene. The United Nations Conference on Environment and Development, Rio De Janeiro, June 1992, demonstrated the world-wide differences based on regional economics. The disagreement between industrialized and developing nations arose over the causes of environmental degradation. Industrialized countries focused on energy efficiency, nontoxic materials and urban greening, while architects from developing countries stressed issues such as poverty, sustainable agriculture and need for political action.

While respecting unique and valid national or regional interests and economics, it must be agreed that the preservation of the natural environment is one of the major issues of todays' world and that there is a need for education and information to consciously help guide the world's future.

Designing interiors is the art of building functional and aesthetically pleasing spaces. However, designing also entails a responsibility which goes beyond what is immediately visible. Through creating living and working spaces, interior designers

shape peoples' life styles, influencing the way they feel, think, and act, affecting their health and comfort.

Since design professionals influence people's lives and shape their behavior, their practice has to represent appropriate ethics. The design has to respond to the environment, take into consideration natural resources, and, in effect, human future. One of the most important aspects of this approach is the idea of sustainability, which accordingly to the World Commission on Environment and Development consists of "meeting the needs of the present without compromising the ability of future generations to meet their own needs." This is a new dimension in the evolving professional ethic of interior designers.

How does this relate to the economy?

"• The potential economic impact of indoor air pollution is quite high; preliminary estimates place potential impacts at tens of billions of dollars per year. Such impacts include direct medical costs and lost earnings due to major illness, as well as increased employee sick days and lost productivity while on the job.

• Labor costs may be 10 to 100 times greater per square foot of office space than energy and other environmental control costs. Where productivity is an important consideration, remedial actions to improve indoor air quality are likely to be cost effective even if they require expensive retrofit" (US EPA, 1989, p.3).

Analyses of project costs cannot be based on the price of the material and labor alone. Even including life cycle costs–costs of maintenance and management–does not really address the real expenses of any project. The remaining environmental costs, which until now have been borne by the public, have to be included, as well, in the price tag.

Interior designers have an unique role and responsibility as the intermediaries between industry and clients. It is up to designers to give information, wake up sensitivity, ask questions and propose solutions. Designers can be instrumental in creating sufficient markets for environmentally safe products. They can convince clients that environmentally sensitive design will improve the occupants' quality of life, comfort and productivity, as well as save operating costs. The savings are often so great that they make up for any initial expense in equipment, materials and systems. The conventional conflict between economy and ecology no longer need apply.

With the market for "green" products growing, industries will be able to lower prices following one of the basic laws of economy: economics of scale. Increased environmental awareness also gives industry the opportunity to develop new markets and improve public relations, as well as to avoid legal costs, taxes and fines for pollution.

Many skeptics challenge proponents of environmentally conscious design to prove the economic benefits of the "greening" of buildings and interiors. Recently there are more and more examples of projects that have proven that intelligent design integrating environmental concerns can be economically sound as well.

"It has become apparent that the lack of social organization, education, training, and political will, are commonly the limiting factors in environmental improvement, rather than a shortage of scientific knowledge" (Southwick, p.117). It is up to interior designers to inform, guide and educate, but first they have to educate themselves.

Part I:
Environmental Issues

"Modern man does not experience himself as a part of nature but as an outside force destined to dominate and conquer it. He even talks of a battle with nature, forgetting that if he won the battle, he would find himself on the losing side. Until quite recently, the battle seemed to go well enough to give him the illusion of unlimited powers, but not so well as to bring the possibility of total victory into view. This has now come into view, and many people, albeit only a minority, are beginning to realize what this means for the continued existence of humanity."

(Schumacher, p.14).

The human impact on the environment grows dangerously with increasing population and with developing, resource-thirsty, technologies. This impact is even more significant in the context of how limited and fragile the Earth's biosphere is. The Earth's biosphere is the Earth's "life zone": a thin and uneven layer capable, in varying degrees, of supporting life. The extent of the earth's biosphere reaches approximately 6 miles beneath the ocean's surface, and approximately as much above. How narrow is this "zone?" It would take a brisk one hour hike in each direction to reach the boundaries. The Earth's total life-support system is also limited by the number of molecules in the planet's surface and in the lowest part of its atmosphere.

Fig. I-1:
Vertical extent of the biosphere .

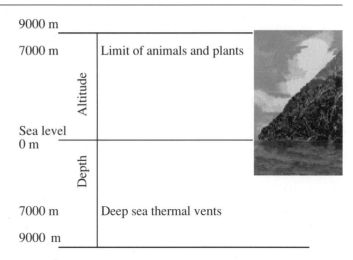

9000 m	
7000 m	Limit of animals and plants
Sea level 0 m	
7000 m	Deep sea thermal vents
9000 m	

Every organism on the Earth affects its environment. The molecules of the Earth's biosphere are constantly involved in recycling processes fueled by energy provided by the Sun. The very definition of ecosystem describes those relations as "self-supporting and self-regulating community of organisms interacting with each other and their environment" (Naar, p.5). But growing human population and developed technologies generate complex and irreversible changes in the Earth's natural ecological balance, changes, which at this time, go beyond the planet's self-healing capability.

Various environmental threats are so tightly interrelated that it is difficult to assess them and establish appropriate responses. Vice President Al Gore, in his book *Earth in the Balance*, suggested classification of environmental threats, using military terminology, into three categories: "local," "regional" and "strategic." With these categories, for example, a polluted river or soil, or illegal waste dumping is a "local" problem. Acid rain or large oil spills which affect vast territories are "regional." The "local" and "regional" problems, by definition, have limited impact, but if they appear simultaneously in many places of the world, they may become threats

to the global balance. An example of such a "strategic" threat would be changes in the Earth's atmosphere.

The first chapter of this part, Global Environment, provides basic information about man-made ecological problems: air pollution and changes in the Earth's atmosphere, water and land pollution, water and soil depletion, and depletion of other natural resources. These are some of the most urgent and crucial environmental threats. They may seem quite remote from an interior designer's everyday practice, while in fact, as is the case with all design industries, the interior designer's decisions have a significant impact on worsening or alleviating the global situation. This book describes these relationships.

The second chapter of this part, Indoor Environment, is devoted to the specific problems of building interiors. As a consequence of design and specified materials and equipment, enclosed spaces can create immediate health hazards for their occupants. This becomes more crucial as people spend more and more time indoors, since the concentration of harmful chemicals in the indoor air can be significantly greater than in open space. Understandably, indoor air quality has become one of the most important issues in today's interior design.

Responsible design solutions that apply to residential and commercial interiors are described in Part II of the book.

CHAPTER 1
GLOBAL ENVIRONMENT

AIR POLLUTION AND THE CHANGES IN EARTH'S ATMOSPHERE

For almost three billion years animals and plants have been recycling and keeping in balance the limited number of air molecules available in the Earth's atmosphere. Nature itself puts great quantities of pollution into the air through, for example, seasonal brush fires or the eruption of volcanoes, but since the early days of the Industrial Revolution, man-made air pollution has begun to produce staggering environmental effects.

Two global effects of air pollution–global warming and ozone depletion–have already become part of today's changes in the Earth's climate and human life condition. "Acid rain" originally could have been considered a local or regional problem. Today, industrial air pollution which causes "acid precipitation," transcends national and regional boundaries and has become a global threat to the environment.

"Greenhouse gases" and global warming

"Greenhouse gases," mainly carbon dioxide, carbon monoxide, and methane, play an important role in determining the temperature of the Earth: they absorb sunlight and infrared radiation, preventing a portion of the heat from radiating back out to space; in other words they trap the sun's heat around the Earth. That heat trapping quality of the surrounding "greenhouse gases" protects the planet's surface from extreme differences in temperature between days and nights, but, when the amount of "greenhouse gases" in the atmosphere rises significantly, the temperature rises as well.

"Greenhouse gases" emissions are created by man's various activities. Burning fossil fuels, clearing land, or making cement from limestone, all produce significant amounts of carbon dioxide. Landfills, cattle raising and growing rice are the main sources of methane. Sulfur dioxide and carbon monoxide are produced by industrial smokestacks and coal fired electric utilities.

The increased amount of heat trapped in the Earth's atmosphere by "greenhouse gases" destroys the natural balance between the amount of energy "coming in" and energy "coming out." This uneven process leads to global warming. Since our planet is a very finely balanced ecosystem, even a change of a few degrees in global temperatures will cause polar ice melting, rise in ocean levels, and climate changes affecting all living organisms.

Side note:
The level of carbon dioxide in the atmosphere has risen in the past 150 years by about 25 percent, and now increases by about 0.5 percent each year. The largest proportion of this increase comes from fuels burned for transportation, electricity generation, heating and industry. Deforestation adds significantly to the level of carbon dioxide. Plants, which kept the balance perfect in a pre-industrial world by acting as natural filters, now can absorb only about 40 percent out of 5 billion tons of carbon dioxide released into the air each year. The atmospheric level of methane, which is even more potent as a greenhouse gas than carbon dioxide, is increasing by about 1 percent each year.

(Source: Global Choices..., pp. 3-4)

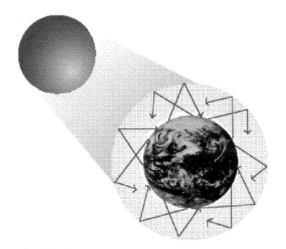

Fig. I-2:
Greenhouse effect: "greenhouse gases" trap heat in the Earth's atmosphere and the amount of the energy "coming in" in the form of sunlight no longer equals the energy "coming out."

Ozone depletion

Ozone is an oxygen molecule that occurs naturally in very small amounts. In the lower atmosphere, ozone is an irritating gas which, in high enough concentrations, can cause irritation of the eyes and mucous membranes. In the earth's upper atmosphere–the stratosphere–ozone absorbs solar

ultraviolet radiation, which otherwise could cause severe damage to all living organisms on the Earth's surface.

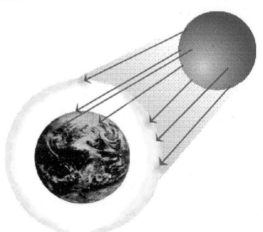

Fig. I-3:
The depleted ozone layer in the upper atmosphere is no longer able to absorb all of the solar ultraviolet radiation and allows more and more of the harmful rays to reach the surface of the Earth.

Under preindustrial conditions the amount of ozone in the lower and upper atmosphere was kept in a healthy equilibrium. Today, due to various technologies and industries, ozone produced in the lower atmosphere contributes to the "greenhouse effect" and pollutes the air. At the same time, ozone is destroyed in the stratosphere, where it has a beneficial effect. Ozone depletion in the upper atmosphere is caused mainly by the release of chlorofluorocarbons (CFCs) into the air. Chlorofluorocarbons do not occur naturally; they were developed in the 1960s. They are very stable chemicals which can last for up to 50 years. CFCs are used primarily for refrigeration and air conditioning. They are also used as blowing agents to produce foamed plastics for insulation, upholstery padding, and packaging, and as propellants for fire extinguishers and aerosols.

In their gas form CFCs drift to the upper atmosphere and destroy ozone molecules. Depletion of ozone in the stratosphere means that more harmful ultraviolet rays reach the surface of the Earth, killing or altering complex molecules in living organisms including DNA. A direct effect on humans is already noticed in southern latitudes: an increased number of skin cancers.

"Acid precipitation"

Burning fossil fuels causes other air pollution beside producing "greenhouse gases." Industrial smokestacks and car tailpipes release millions of tons of sulfur and nitrogen oxides (SO_2 and NO_x). These gases turn into sulfuric and nitric acids when in contact with water.

Emitted from industrial smokestacks, both sulfur and nitrogen oxides rise to high altitudes. From there, depending on weather patterns and winds, this chemical brew is carried hundreds and thousands of miles, interacting with water vapor and producing dilute acids droplets that fall to Earth. The increase of the acidity of soils and water greatly stresses vegetation and fisheries, threatening natural and agricultural resources, endangering human health, causing destruction of metals, masonry and marble on buildings.

Fig. I-4:
Arch of Septimus Severus on Roman Forum in Rome "melting" under the influence of pollution.
(Photo: Author.)

"At the heart of the acid-rain controversy is the fact that the components of acid rain are created in regions economically dependent on 'smokestack' industries that produce the pollution, while the effects are experienced in regions that get much of their income from tourism, agriculture, and forest products, all of which depend on a clean environment" (Naar, p.102). The building of tall smokestacks for power plants and other industries is a good example of a short-term solution to the local problem that, in turn, produced a more severe long-term threat. Tall smokestacks were supposed to reduce air pollution in the immediate area of factories and plants through releasing their dirty gases into higher altitudes. In turn, they aggravate the problem, since the longer the oxides remain in cloud layers, the more acid is formed.

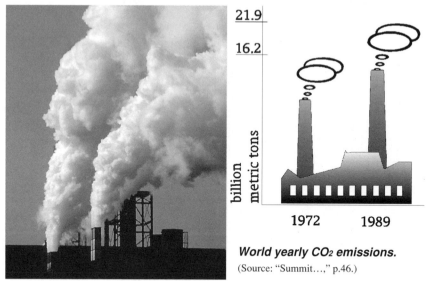

Fig. I-5:
Steel plant in Ohio, USA.
(Photo: © Robert Visser, Greenpeace, 1993.)

World yearly CO_2 emissions.
(Source: "Summit…," p.46.)

Sulfur dioxide and oxides of nitrogen have been proven to damage vegetation. Oxides of nitrogen, in addition, directly threaten the quality of human life: they irritate the respiratory membranes and are health hazards, especially for children.

Limiting emissions of "greenhouse gases" along with sulfur and nitrogen oxides is one of the most important steps in preventing drastic climate and atmospheric changes. The least costly way of limiting emissions is by increasing energy efficiency and, where possible, employing clean sources of energy. To lower the demand on energy, interior designers should specify energy efficient lighting and appliances, adequate insulation, and the use of natural light and natural ventilation in their designs. It is also important that designers specify materials which require less energy to manufacture and transport, and use recycled products, which themselves are also recyclable. Consumption of energy can be decreased and the strain on the environment lowered without sacrificing comfort, security or aesthetics of homes, offices, or public spaces.

The international Montreal Protocol was signed in 1987 to stop all the production of CFCs by the year 2000, but the effects of chemicals already produced will last for many more years. To alleviate the impact of CFCs, interior designers in their practice should avoid specifying, therefore promoting, the use of materials and mechanical systems which require CFCs in either the manufacturing or the operating processes.

Side note:
"In terms of amount emitted in the United States, carbon monoxide is the number-one air pollutant and the automobile by far the major source. However in terms of human health, sulfur dioxide and particulates rank as the top two offenders" (Naar, p.82).

WATER POLLUTION AND DEPLETION

Changes in the global atmosphere – global warming and acid precipitation – have a direct impact on the quantity and quality of water. Climate changes can bring devastating turns in weather patterns and lead to desertification or floods. Acid precipitation causes acidification of waters, in many cases to the point that they are not able to support vegetation or fisheries or any other life form.

Side note:
"Lakes, ponds, and streams are the first victims [of acid rain], especially where bedrock and soils are low in carbonates and similar chemicals that can neutralize acids. Thousands of lakes in the northeastern United States, Canada, and Scandinavia are so acidic that fish cannot live in them. A 1988 report by the University of Massachusetts Water Resources center revealed more acid-rain damage in that state already than the EPA forecasts for the entire Northeast in 50 years. In Sweden and Norway a majority of the streams and lakes are technically 'dead' or on the critical list" (Naar, p.99).

Side note:
Our use of paper, which is estimated at 250 pounds per year per person, contributes 4 to 8 tons of highly toxic chlorine used for bleaching being released every day by paper mills ("Global choices...," p.7).

The list of the most typical pollutants dumped into the oceans and rivers is long and includes chemicals from various industries and mines, oil spills from tankers or offshore drilling rigs, radioactive wastes, garbage and sewage. Even agriculture contributes to water pollution through the runoff of pesticides, herbicides and fertilizers. In addition, industry, especially the electric-power industry, discharges great amounts of waste heat into water. Such thermal pollution may trigger biological and chemical reactions which would not normally occur in a natural environment. It may also raise the temperature above the level tolerable for fish.

The major industries which account for a large portion of waste water discharge include the paper, chemical, petroleum, and steel industries. For example, every time a designer specifies a ton of steel, he/she also specifies the consumption of 37 tons of water (Vale and Vale, p.37). Another interior design related industry notorious for water waste and pollution is the textile industry. The production of textiles requires extensive use of water in fiber production, in processing fibers and in fabric finishing especially in dyeing. In residential use, only approximately 5 percent of water is actually used for direct consumption; the remaining 95 percent is used just to transport waste (Brown et al., p.195).

The attitude of industrialized nations toward water supplies is reminiscent of the attitude toward electricity and oil before the 1970s energy crisis. Most developed nations dismiss the fact that world resources of water are limited. Supplies of drinking water, which decrease along with the growth in world population, ground water pollution, and overconsumption, are declining particularly rapidly. From 1950 to 1980, the world's use of water rose from about 10 percent to 50 percent of the planet's available annual water supply. If the rate of increase in both population and per-person water use continues, the planet's capacity will be exceeded within ten to twenty years.

The quality of drinking water is a cause for growing concern in the United States. According to *The Progressive Review*, 20 percent of groundwater used for drinking in the USA is contaminated. In rural areas, groundwater has been contaminated by pesticides, cleaning solvents and seepage from landfills. In urban areas, the main problem is caused by the level of chlorine added to prevent bacterial contamination. The chlorine has side effects: bad tasting water and the deterioration of pipes and plumbing fixtures. Increased amounts of chemicals absorbed through drinking and washing can accumulate in the human body and become a health hazard.

Side note:
"Acid rain's indirect impact on health is caused by its increasing the corrosiveness of surface and ground water. When this water gets into your water supply, it can leach out toxic metals and asbestos from watersheds, sediments, and plumbing into the water you drink. This is particularly dangerous when the pipes are themselves made, even in small part, of toxic metals. A recent survey of 158 Massachusetts municipal drinking waters found that 73 percent were extremely 'aggressive'–i.e. able to corrode metals from piping systems" (Naar, p.100).

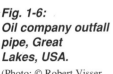

Fig. 1-6:
Oil company outfall pipe, Great Lakes, USA.
(Photo: © Robert Visser, Greenpeace, 1988.)

LAND AND SOIL DEGRADATION AND POLLUTION

Man-induced pollution of air and water, the development of extensive transportation routes, megacities, technology-supported agriculture, all take an active role in the destruction of land. Among the most dangerous threats to the land, soil erosion and problems caused by solid waste are the most immediate.

Soil erosion

Climatic changes, pollution and poor agricultural practices often lead to the destruction of top soil, and in extreme cases, to the total degradation of land. Soil erosion is a natural process, but when, for whatever reason, soil erosion exceeds the rate of new soil formation, the land's inherent productivity begins to decline. First, the natural vegetation is disrupted by clearing of trees, overgrazing, monocultures of a single crop and other harmful agricultural activities. Then, water and wind erode topsoil. What often follows, especially in arid, semi-arid and other sensitive zones of the earth, is desertification–the development of desert-like conditions. The most vivid examples of such effects of human practices include the destruction of tropical rain forests in South America and desertification of the Sahel region in Africa.

Extremely exploitative agricultural practices leading to soil erosion are usually the effect of short-sighted policies, directly connected with social and economic problems of poor regions and countries.

Interior designers should be aware and remember that:

• Many exotic species of trees used in the furniture industry come from rain forests in poor regions of the world for which they provide immediate, although short-lived, income at the expense of total destruction of fragile top soil. The complex issue of the effects of deforestation will be described in the next section;

• Natural fibers, such as cotton, require intensive use of fertilizers and pesticides which contribute significantly to soil pollution.

Solid waste

"Some environmental problems can be worked out between government regulators and affected industries themselves. Solid waste is not one of them. [People] have direct control over trash through what they purchase and what they throw away. The amount of waste generated, the toxicity of material discarded, and the level of recycling and waste reduction are all affected by citizen decisions."

(Goldstein and Izeman, p.4).

The main source of land and soil pollution, besides agricultural use of pesticides and fertilizers, is solid waste. Agricultural, mineral, residential and industrial solid waste affects air and water, but the first victim is the land.

Waste is a problem that will not go away by itself. The US Environmental Protection Agency estimates that almost twice as much trash was recycled or composted in 1990 as in 1985, but still by the year 1995 half of our present landfill areas will be filled to capacity.

Side note:
"Building products–indeed most consumer products–are simply made in such a way that it is difficult for nature to reintegrate or "digest" them once the human species find that they are no longer useful" (Wagner, "Visionary...," p.55).

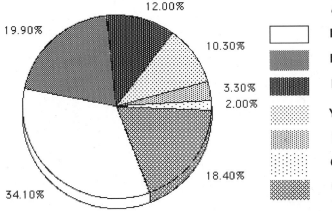

Fig. I-7:
Content of a landfill in percent of each category:

Paper

Plastics

Metal

Yard waste

Food

Glass

Other

(Source: "Finding...", p.1.)

Side note:

Over the past few decades the technology of landfilling has improved. To prevent wastes from getting into groundwater, the bottoms of newer landfills are being sealed with heavy plastic liners. Drainage systems have reduced infiltration of water, limiting the danger of chemicals being leached through the trash levels. Each day's trash deposits are covered with a layer of soil to help control problems with rodents, birds, blowing debris and odors. Methane is being collected by the network of pipes buried in the layers of trash. The collected gas is, in some cases, used to generate steam and electricity. But even those improvements do not change the reality that resources, including energy used to produce discarded materials, are being forever removed from the utilization (Lyle, pp.225-226).

Under the dominant pattern of consumption, virtually every pound of natural resources taken from fields, forests, mines or wells ends up sooner or later either in a landfill, or in some other form of pollution. Each person in the USA produces 50,000 pounds of solid waste each year (Lyle, p. 225). Besides the fact that there is no space for new landfills, existing sites cause serious problems. The two major forms of pollution originating from landfills are leachate and methane. Leachate is rainwater which filters through a landfill site, collects toxic contaminants, and often passes into surrounding waters and groundwater. Methane is a gas produced from the decomposition of refuse and one of the most potent substances contributing to global warming.

The way of dealing with solid waste which appeals to many decision makers is incineration. "It comes closer than any other technology to simply making waste disappear..." (Lyle, p. 226). The "lure" of incineration is that it reduces the volume of materials that have to be landfilled without making basic changes in existing waste-disposal procedures. Incineration can also generate energy and provide job opportunities. But the disadvantages of incineration are quite serious and include high cost,

Fig. I-8:
The biggest man-made structure in the world: Fresh Kill Landfill on Staten Island, NY.
(Photo: H.Pancewicz.)

toxic ash residue, the difficulty of controling air pollution and the fact that too many materials cannot be burned.

Interior designers, as well as other professionals involved in the construction industry, contribute significantly to this alarming situation. Building practices are costly and wasteful. More than 10 percent of landfill waste comes from the construction industry. The bulk of it is from demolitions, which often involve useful buildings being replaced with new, due to economic shifts in urban land value. Reduction of construction waste involves the recycling of a whole building and/or part of the materials, as well as thoughtful use of new materials, management of discarded packaging and use of recycled and recyclable materials and products.

Side note:
Demolition waste contains thousands of sinks, tubs, doors and windows which could be reused (if they weren't damaged during the demolition itself) or recycled.

Fig. I-9:
Construction waste from one new home equals 2.5 tons and includes:

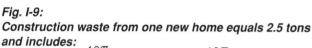
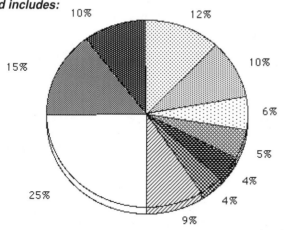
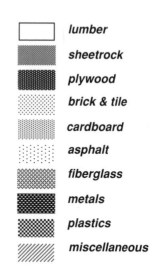

- lumber
- sheetrock
- plywood
- brick & tile
- cardboard
- asphalt
- fiberglass
- metals
- plastics
- miscellaneous

In contrast typical major residential renovation including new walls, flooring, plumbing, wiring, painting and roofing saves:
• About 120 cubic yards of landfill (5 large truck-loads);
• Enough energy (for the production of new materials) to operate the house for 4.5 years;
• From $15 to $40 per square foot in construction costs.   (Source: "Global choices...," p. 9.)

DEPLETION OF OTHER RESOURCES

"Economic deficits may dominate our headlines, but ecological deficits will dominate our future. Accounting systems signal when a country begins to run up an economic deficit, but they do not indicate when the sustainable yield threshold of a biological resource, such as a forest, has been crossed. Ecological deficits such as loss of tree cover or of topsoil often go unnoticed until they begin to affect economic indicators. But by that time, excessive demand may be consuming the resource itself, converting a renewable resource into a nonrenewable one."

(Brown, p.8).

Natural resources are the base for the productivity and economy of every region in the world. The supplies or shortages of natural resources are so critical for the survival of every nation that they create tensions, political conflicts, and even lead to the wars. Development of technologies allowing sustainable utilization of natural resources will decide the future of the world. In the *Worldwatch Institute Report, State of the World 1986*, L. R. Brown lists six main resources whose extent of depletion is already adversely affecting global economy: forests, grasslands, fisheries, soil, water, and oil.

The distinction between nonrenewable and renewable resources is based on the possibility of regeneration. A nonrenewable resource is a resource whose supply in the world is finite, or limited, or depleted to such a degree that its recovery is cost prohibitive. Examples of nonrenewable resources include ores, minerals, and fossil fuels. A renewable resource is essentially unlimited in supply. The only

resource which totally fulfills this definition is energy from the sun. Otherwise the term is used to describe resources, for example plants, which can be relatively easily re-created. But, if the demand on a renewable resource constantly exceeds the sustainable yield, then the reproductive capacity of this resource is limited and an ecological deficit occurs. If the demand continues, this may lead to the total collapse of supplies. This is already the reality of forest and grasslands deficits throughout Africa, the Middle East, India, and Central America. If the rate of natural resources exploitation remains at today's level, the price for the diminished resource base will be paid by the next generation.

A closer look at the nonrenewable nature of today's main energy sources and at the complex issue of deforestation provides convincing examples of the extent of resource depletion and illustrates the complex interrelation between environmental threats.

Fossil fuels

The energy crisis in the 1970s brought world attention to the fact that almost all of the productive energy in the world is drawn from nonrenewable resources. Fossil fuels, including coal and oil, are products of the natural processes accumulating over centuries, and their supplies are finite. "Only a fixed quantity is available and that quantity is not renewable. Once extracted from the ground and transformed into their many by-products, these energy resources cannot be re-created; they are exhaustible" (Harf, p. 27). In addition, today's main sources of energy–fossil fuels–create most of the environmental problems: mining displaces habitats; oil spills destroy beaches and species of the affected marine environment, air pollution devastates forest

and causes climatic changes that can disrupt food production, reduce dependable water supplies, and jeopardize coastal cities and towns.

Until technology for clean and sustainable energy is developed and widely applied, the most effective measure of preserving existing resources and lowering the strain on the environment is designing for energy efficiency.

Deforestation

"The destruction of tropical forests is a headline story throughout the world.... On the surface, the solution for curbing deforestation seems simple enough: stop cutting down trees. However, the problems of deforestation are much more complex."
(Hammel, p.24)

The devastating impact of excessive demand on natural resources may be understood through the study of forest depletion. The destruction of forests influences water distribution, air quality, soil productivity, and the functioning of the whole ecosystem in the regions affected. Harvested by lumber and paper industries, cleared for agriculture, gathered for firewood, damaged by acid precipitation and other pollution, forests of the world are collapsing under the accelerating destruction.

According to the United Nations Food and Agriculture Organization (FAO), the rain forest belt, located around the Equator, in Latin and South America, Africa and Southeast Asia, is being destroyed at a rate of 40 million to 50 million acres annually–the land size of Italy. At the present rate of destruction the Earth's rain forests will be gone by the year 2050.

Side note:
"The depletion of forests, which began with a chipped flint hand-axe, has led to changes in water levels, massive erosion of soil and loss of plant and animal life, as habitats are violated due to ignorance, greed, or just thoughtlessness without malice"(Holdsworth, p. 20).

Further complicating the issue is the fact that many of the rare woods come from poverty-burdened, developing countries. If woods are not harvested as a cash crop, they may be cleared to make way for crops that will bring more profit. As much as half of the rain forest areas cleared each year is cleared by landless farmers for shifting cultivation. The fastest way of accomplishing this is through burning of all the vegetation on the chosen piece of land. In addition to the total destruction, this process releases carbon dioxide and oxides of nitrogen into the atmosphere. Sometimes even the rare woods are used for fuel. Modern logging techniques are increasingly damaging: loggers may take only a few prime trees from a forest, but their road construction and their heavy machinery kill or damage many other trees.

Fig. I-10:
Floodplain logging in rain forest in Brazil.

(Photo: © Plowden, Greenpeace, 1989.)

Studies have shown that tropical forest destruction affects regional, as well as the global climates. Trees are the most efficient converters of carbon dioxide and water into cellulose–they act as "cleaning filters" for the atmosphere. Trees influence the earth's surface energy balance by reflecting sunlight, evaporating water, and drawing

groundwater up through their roots. Irresponsible deforestation contributes in many ways to global climatic changes and especially to global warming through the greenhouse effect.

In addition, with forests being lost, the process called "genetic erosion," a reduction within all living species, increases every year. It is estimated that globally we lose more than one animal or plant species a day: "An estimate ... suggests that between half a million and 2 million species–15 to 20 percent of all species on earth–could be extinguished by 2000, mainly because of loss of wild habitat but also in part because of pollution. Extinction of species on this scale is without precedent in Human history." (Southwick, p.50). Many rain forest plants, birds, fishes, insects, reptiles, four-footed animals, and other living organisms have not yet been researched, or cataloged. The greatest biological diversity, its beneficial attributes and scientific values are destroyed without even taking a note.

Fig. I-11:
Ring-tailed lemur.
(Photo: author.)

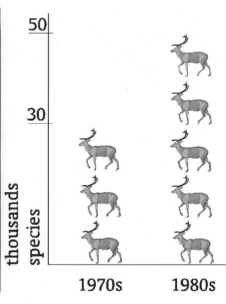

World yearly extinction rate of species. (Source: "Summit...," p.51.)

Deforestation is not limited to the rain forest. In the United States about 90 percent of old growth has been destroyed. Currently, forests in North America are consumed at a faster rate than in Brazil. North American forests are as vulnerable as any other environment. Tree planting practices have been mainly geared toward replanting single species, which can not replace original growth; as virgin forests were destroyed, unique habitats were lost. Soil, water, plants and wildlife, which play a significant and interconnecting role within the ecosystem, are all affected by degrading activities. In some cases, degradation is so severe that the ecosystem ceases to function altogether.

Fig. I-12:
Clear-cutting in Washington State.
(Photo: © Plowden, Greenpeace, 1982.)

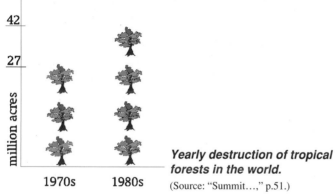

Yearly destruction of tropical forests in the world.
(Source: "Summit...," p.51.)

In developed countries, forests are also destroyed by industrial pollution. The deterioration of forests in California, the Midwest and Northeastern USA and in most of Europe has been mainly caused by acid precipitation. "It ... has been identified as a prime cause of waldsterben (tree death) affecting more than half of the forests in West Germany and those in southern Sweden, Switzerland, and the U.K.... Acid rain presents a triple threat to forests: it prevents nutrients from reaching trees through their leaves; it leaches nutrients out of the root zone; and it concentrates aluminum in the soil, which can block the roots' uptake of vital magnesium and calcium. These attacks can work alone or in combination. When a tree loses nutrients in its foliage, it tries to compensate by taking up more from the soil. And, if these are not available, the tree becomes more susceptible to damage from frost and insects" (Naar, p.99).

The economics of the situation, however, demand a sensitive reaction. For example, banning or boycotting all tropical timber or wood products could easily destroy the economic incentive for preserving such forests. Nonprofit environmental study groups, such as Earth Access, have identified some rainforest woods that can be used by responsible designers since they come from sustainable forestry programs.

· · ·

In describing environmental impacts, attention usually is focused on raw materials or on final products, but to make proper judgments, the whole production process needs to be considered. To evaluate a product, it is necessary to have information about the manufacturing technology of the product including air, water or soil use and pollution; the

extent of energy required to manufacture, transport and install; and the use of recycled materials, packaging, and so on. For example, "A paper manufacturer whose products contain 100 percent recycled fiber but whose manufacturing processes release dioxin will find itself in an environmental dilemma" (Wagner, "How to...," p.72). It is also important to consider the impact that a manufacturing process has on the health of factory workers, as well as how some of the products may influence the health of the construction crew during their installation.

Additional information

More in-depth analysis can be found in:

Gore, Al. *Earth in the Balance: Ecology and the Human Spirit.* New York: Penguin Books USA Inc., 1993.

Harf, James E. *The Politics of Global Resources; Population, Food, Energy, and Environment.* Durham, NC: Duke University Press, 1986.

Naar, Jon. *Design for a Livable Planet: How You Can Help Clean Up the Environment.* New York: Harper & Row, 1990

Schumacher, E. F. *Small Is Beautiful. Economics as if People Mattered.* New York: Harper and Row, 1973.

Southwick, Charles H. *Global Ecology.* Sunderland, MA: Sinauer Associates, 1985.

CHAPTER 2
INDOOR ENVIRONMENT

The environmental changes and threats discussed in Chapter 1 are influenced by the way buildings and interiors are constructed, equipped, used and maintained. Materials used in construction and in furnishing interiors often come from depleted resources. Some of them require manufacturing processes notorious for air and water pollution, or energy use. Many materials and products have to be transported from far away. Finished buildings themselves are sources of extensive pollution (inefficient HVAC systems, lack of provisions for recycling), or wasteful in use of resources (energy, water, etc.). The concept of sustainable interiors, that is, interiors designed in such a manner that they sensibly address the impact of all their functions, parts and elements on the global environment, is discussed at length throughout the rest of this book. But there is one other significant environmental issue, exclusive to enclosed spaces, which directly affects and influences the health and well-being of building occupants: indoor air quality (IAQ).

The deciding factors in indoor air quality are the various sources of indoor air pollution and the design, operation and maintenance of building ventilation systems.

INDOOR AIR POLLUTION

The problem of air pollution–harmful gases or particles released into the air–is more serious inside than outside, in part because some of the chemicals indoors have concentrations 100 times greater than might ever be encountered in open spaces. The issue has become even more critical since the 1970s energy crisis. At that time, as energy prices climbed,

building managers began to insulate buildings by sealing windows and closing air-intake ducts to save energy. In effect, they trapped stale and contaminated air indoors, causing a rise in pollution and, subsequently, health-related problems. Indoor air pollution is one of the most serious environmental problem in the USA also because, according to the EPA, Americans spend almost 90 percent of their time indoors.

The term coined in recent years to describe the situation existing in many buildings is "sick building syndrome" (SBS). It defines a building in which occupants complain of health and comfort problems–respiratory problems, irritation, and fatigue–related to being or working in this building. SBS describes specific problems related to indoor air pollution, not to inadequate temperature or humidity control, although high temperature and high humidity levels may increase concentrations of some pollutants.

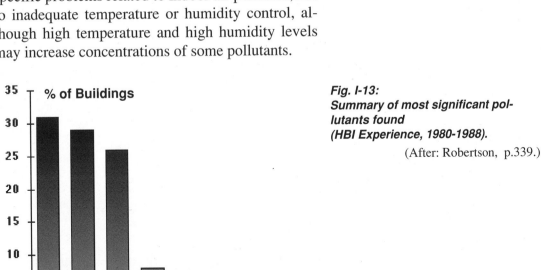

Fig. I-13:
Summary of most significant pollutants found
(HBI Experience, 1980-1988).

(After: Robertson, p.339.)

There are two main sources of indoor pollution: building related and occupant related. Building related pollution may originate from exterior sources, the building's materials and finishes, construction methods, HVAC systems, or maintenance problems. Occupant related air pollution is unavoidable, since pollutants include products of human biological activity. "Virtually everything we use in buildings sheds particulate matter and/or produces gases" (Robertson, p.334). People shed millions of particles, primarily skin scales, and contribute significant amounts of carbon dioxide. Cleaning, cooking, broiling, gas and oil burning, personal hygiene, smoking, all generate airborne particulates, vapors and gases.

Microbial contamination

The term "microbial contamination" describes harmful microbes that originate from people, plants, food, and all possible organic debris. These microbes are nourished by normal indoor warmth and humidity and may cause objectionable odors. According to the World Health Organization, 40 percent of all so-called "sick buildings" are contaminated by such microscopic growth.

There are two main types of microbial contamination: bacteria and fungi. The best known examples of bacteria responsible for human infections include Salmonella and Legionnaire's disease, both of which, in extreme situations, can and do cause death. Fungi usually take the form of mold and mildew capable of producing microscopic spores that contribute to respiratory problems as well as causing odors.

Contaminated central air systems, lack of proper ventilation, high levels of humidity, incorrectly specified building and interior materials or finishes (e.g., placing carpet nonresistant to moisture in a high moisture area), all can trigger the breeding conditions for these contaminants.

Volatile organic compounds (VOCs)

Volatile organic compounds are invisible and sometimes odorless fumes or vapors, associated with almost any man-made or natural product in a confined space: plywood, plastics, fibers, varnishes, coatings, cleaning chemicals, and so on. VOCs evaporate from buildings and furnishing products; they originate from solvents used in paints, waxes, and consumer products or petroleum fuels. Many of these chemicals, which can easily turn to gas at room temperature, are toxic and can affect the central nervous system, provoking physical symptoms (typically eye and respiratory system related) or psychological irritation. Some of VOCs are detectable by their sharp odors; others require sensitive instruments to detect.

The most widespread VOC, formaldehyde, is a major contributor to sick building syndrome and has become a prototype in research because of its clearly demonstrated negative effect on people with chemical sensitivities. Formaldehyde can be found in interior-grade plywood or particleboard, in medium density fiberboard, in insulation and in some textiles. Formaldehyde, which evaporates as an odorless gas, is used as a disinfectant, preservative, hardener, and synthesizing agent. When released from these sources, formaldehyde can cause irritation to eyes and lungs, and some researchers believe it to be a potential carcinogen. Effects of formaldehyde can last a few hours or for many years after installation of materials but are most severe when materials are new.

Side note:
The opinions about how harmful VOCs are can be quite controversial. Anthony King, President of Axcess Marketing Group, Inc., in his article in IBD/NY Newsletter writes: "VOCs, per se, are neither good nor bad; they're a natural by-product of all organic compounds–things containing a combination of the elements carbon and hydrogen. The pungent smell of freshly mowed grass is a VOC. The prestigious aroma of a new car interior is likewise a VOC–in fact, the concentrated off-gassing of plastics, leathers, and fabrics in a sealed compartment" (King, p. 7).

Other VOCs include:
• Xylenes and toluene–petrochemicals found in various adhesives and solvents;
• Styrene–possible carcinogen present in many paints, plastic foams, plastics and resins;
• Benzene–carcinogen found in cigarette smoke, paints and other finishes;
• Ethyl benzene–compound causing severe irritation to eyes and respiratory tract, found in various solvents.

There are many other VOCs, but, in many cases, the insufficient research does not allow for determining the direct effects of exposure to them.

"What adds to unpredictable effects is that building materials appear to act as a sponge for VOCs, taking contaminants in, and then releasing them later, often in a new chemical form, since they can mix with indigenous pollutants already in the material" (Holdsworth and Sealey, p.63). Research done in Sweden in 1988 proved that a lot of the VOCs initially released from furnishing or finishes are absorbed onto high-surface-area materials, such as carpeting, ceiling tiles, or free standing partitions. The quantities of VOCs absorbed depend on the total surface area and on the air exchange rate in the space. Rougher surfaces (textiles, carpets, etc.) absorb higher quantities of VOCs. The lower the ventilation rate, the more VOCs are absorbed on interior surfaces. Also the higher the temperature, the higher the emissions and VOC air concentrations (Holdsworth and Sealey, pp. 63-64).

The ultimate goal is not necessarily the total elimination of VOCs from indoor air, since spaces are occupied by people, and people are one of the sources of VOCs. What is necessary is awareness and management of VOCs. They can be managed by limiting sources and by proper ventilation, which includes the control of humidity and of air exchange. In some cases, high levels of toxic or harmful VOCs in products require more drastic actions, perhaps even a ban on the use and production of such products.

Products of chemical reactions

Chemical reactions of concern include: combustion, human metabolism and smoking. Their most common products include:
- Nitrogen oxide (NO_x)–a yellowish brown gas, product of tobacco smoke and combustion; it interferes with breathing and can cause lung damage;
- Carbon monoxide (CO)–an odorless gas, product of combustion, often present near garages, combustion equipment, or in indoor air contaminated by tobacco smoke; it interferes with oxygen intake and can be life threatening;
- Carbon dioxide (CO2)–an odorless gas, product of complete carbon combustion in machines and in human metabolism; although always present in the air, at concentrations above 10,000 parts per million carbon dioxide can cause loss of mental acuity.

The presence of these gases is usually related to activities in the space or spillage from garage or mechanical rooms. If the outbreak is acute, especially of carbon monoxide, it may require immediate action including, in extreme cases, evacuation of the building.

One of the most common sources of indoor chemical pollutants is tobacco smoke. Environmental tobacco smoke (ETS) is a mixture of irritating gases and carcinogenic tar particles. Cigarette smoke contains more than 4700 chemical

Side note:
According to Gray Robertson of Healthy Buildings International, Inc., ETS is blamed for poor indoor air quality and associated effects primarily because it is one of the few indoor pollutants that can be seen and smelled. The NIOSH has reported that only 2% of the poor air quality in the investigated buildings was attributable to environmental tobacco smoke. The leading cause for most of the office workers' complaints in the buildings researched by HBI was inadequate ventilation. In fact, ventilation experts frequently gauge the operational efficiency of ventilation systems by using smoke tests. If smoke persists, it is an indication that a serious ventilation problem exists. But it is easier and less expensive to post "No smoking" signs then to improve a deficient ventilation system.

compounds including carbon monoxide, nicotine, carcinogenic tars, and sulfur dioxide. According to the NRC, short-term exposure most likely can cause irritation to the eyes, nose, or throat; prolonged exposure to ETS may lead to more serious health problems. In answer to the alarming research concerning the carcinogenic character of ETS, smoking in many public spaces today is restricted or totally eliminated. "There is no known 'safe level' of exposure to a cancer-causing agent" (Agran, p.33).

Electromagnetic fields

Today's global society is fueled by electromagnetic energy and there is really no place to hide from it at home or at work. Public attention has focused largely on electric utility lines, but in fact, visual display terminals (VDTs) present a source of radiation far in excess of the fields associated with electric distribution wires.

Electromagnetic fields (EMF) are a form of radiation present whenever electricity runs through a wire or an appliance. The movement of the electric current creates a magnetic field; the stronger the electric current the stronger the magnetic field. Among those elements affecting electromagnetic fields in buildings, the most common are: electrical wiring and appliances, a history of pesticide use, dampness and fumes from oil-fired heaters. "Like many other 'factors of influence' it may well be that the greatest danger is from a combination of individual sources, each having some factor of risk—but considered at this present time to be low and 'acceptable'. Put together they could provide a lethal cocktail that may prove hard to analyze" (Holdsworth and Sealey, p.71).

Initially, researchers studying the potential harmful effects on employees focused on ionizing radiation, such as the X-rays from VDTs. Now, however,

research has shown that the levels of ionizing radiation are very low, and it is virtually impossible for such rays to penetrate through the VDT screen. More recently, the attention has shifted to nonionizing radiation from VDTs, such as electromagnetic rays.

The EPA has prepared a review of the available scientific literature concerning EMF (US EPA "Evaluation…"), which states that there is "…a possible but not proven, cause of cancer in humans." Several studies have established an association between magnetic fields and an increased incidence of cancer, while another study has observed a heightened risk of miscarriage among women who used VDTs more than 20 hours per week during the first trimester of pregnancy (Malino and Lee, p. 74).

Although research is not conclusive concerning the effects of exposure to electromagnetic radiation, some animal studies have suggested that such radiation at VDT frequencies can have a biological effect on the animal. It is then possible to conclude that humans also could be affected. With the enormous growth of VDT usage throughout the office environment today, statisticians argue that chance alone could account for these relatively small numbers of negative health effects.

In addition, stress associated with poorly planned VDT work environments, including inadequate lighting, poor ergonomic design, overcrowding, poor ventilation and diverse indoor pollutants, increases the health risks among people working for long hours on VDTs.

Other indoor toxins and pollutants

There are other indoor toxins and pollutants that interior designers should be aware of, although in most cases, their control falls within the architect's responsibility.

Side note:
"It is not radon itself that poses the greatest threat to people, but the so-called radon-daughter products. Radon decays through a succession of decay products, producing metallic ions. These decay products then attach themselves to particles suspended in the air. When inhaled these decay products rest in the respiratory tract. The subsequent decay produces alpha particles which increase the health risk" (Holdsworth and Sealey, p.38).

Side note:
"Intact and undisturbed asbestos materials do not pose a health risk" (US EPA, "Building...," p.147).

• **Radon**

Radon is a radioactive gas produced by the decay of radioactive uranium, which occurs naturally in the soil, groundwater and air. Radon can cause an increased risk of lung cancer for people who are exposed to relatively high concentrations over a long period of time. Radon can move from the soil by diffusion into air pockets or water. "It has been estimated by some researchers that anywhere from 10 to 15 percent of the radon we are exposed to comes from water used indoors" (Robertson, p.335).

Radon can be controlled by the proper sealing of foundations and floor slabs. Testing for radon can be done through local health departments or EPA offices.

• **Asbestos**

Asbestos is a group of six naturally occurring, mineral silicate fibers. It is perhaps the most familiar and most publicized of all interior health hazards. Known since ancient times for its resistance to fire, asbestos fiber achieved commercial importance in the 19th century. It was used as a structural fire-resistant coating and can often be found in duct or furnace insulation in homes built prior to 1978. Asbestos was also used in acoustic tile, ceiling and floor coverings, and many other building materials. The fiber usually appears as a white, light gray or light brown coarse fabric or paper, or as a dense pulpy mass of light gray "stucco like" material applied to ceilings, beams and columns. Unless the material is damaged or disturbed, there is little health risk.

When disturbed, asbestos separates into very thin fibers that are invisible to the naked eye and that may remain in the air for many hours. People who are exposed to high levels of airborne asbestos have an increased risk of contracting a wide range of respiratory illnesses. Because of this, asbestos removal

is potentially dangerous and should be undertaken only by a professional, licensed asbestos contractor. "EPA and NIOSH recommend a practical approach that protects public health by emphasizing that ACM [asbestos-containing material] in buildings should be identified and appropriately managed, and that those workers who might disturb it should be properly trained and protected" (US EPA, "Building...," p.148).

• **Lead**

Lead has been known and used for over 5000 years. The ancient civilizations of Phoenicia, Egypt, Greece, India, China, and later the Romans used lead for vessels, water ducts, utensils, and so on. In modern times this common industrial metal can be found in some paint and paint particles, lead solder, automobile exhaust, improperly glazed dishes, leaded crystal and lead foil on wine bottles. Since it is neurotoxic and cumulative, lead is most dangerous to fetuses, infants and children. It is easily absorbed into their growing bodies and can cause learning and behavior problems.

Houses built before 1950 are the most likely to contain paint with high levels of lead. Many interiors of homes have woodwork and walls painted with lead-based paint. They should not be sanded or burned off. Moldings or other woodwork should be replaced or chemically treated. Removal of lead-based paint should be done by a professional, licensed contractor.

• **Ozone**

Ozone is an irritating, pale blue gas composed of three oxygen atoms (O_3). Ozone is explosive and toxic, even at low concentrations. It occurs naturally in very small amounts in the Earth's stratosphere. Under certain conditions, photochemical reactions

between nitrogen oxides and hydrocarbons can produce ozone in concentrations high enough to cause irritation to the eyes and mucous membranes. Ozone usually is manufactured by passing an electric discharge through a current of oxygen or dry air.

The risk of indoor ozone pollution is the highest in small, badly ventilated offices equipped with photocopiers and laser printers. Even a relatively minute presence of 0.1 ozone part per million is enough to cause irritation to eyes and breathing systems. Increased levels can cause nausea, headaches and increased risk of lung infection.

VENTILATION

Indoor pollution builds up when the sources of pollution are excessive or when ventilation is inadequate. Pollution can be limited by the proper choice of materials, but even more by proper design and maintenance of the ventilation system. According to NIOSH there are three major causes of sick building syndrome: poor ventilation, inadequate filtration, and contamination.

The problem of poor ventilation became acute in the 1970s when energy conservation concerns limited the quantity of fresh air entering buildings. Many building owners and operators closed air-intake dampers, sealed up the windows and cracks forcing occupants to breathe only recycled air. In fact, with more tightly sealed buildings, it is necessary to provide for increased frequency of air exchanges and increased intake of fresh air from outside.

Both the outside air and recycled air has to be filtered. Inadequate filtration can be caused by low efficiency filters, or filters which are installed improperly, torn, clogged, and so on, all of which render them ineffective, or in the worst cases, virtually useless.

Fig. I-14:
Sick building syndrome causes: HBI Experience,
1980 -1988

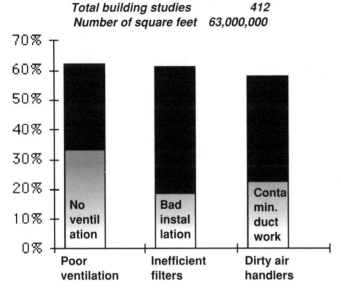

| Total building studies | 412 |
| Number of square feet | 63,000,000 |

(After: Robertson, p.339.)

Fresh and processed air travels through long ducts. "Air conditioning systems–often consisting of miles of ductwork–are often prime breeding grounds for bacteria, molds and fungi, many of which can cause illness and even death. Remarkably, ductwork tends to be installed without any provision for subsequent access or cleaning. This out-of-sight, out-of-mind mentality often leads to a massive build-up of ductwork contamination that is spread to building occupants as air passes through the ductwork" (Robertson, p.340). Providing access to all ductwork may not be possible due to construction or design; this means that the quality of the indoor air has to depend even more on installation of appropriate filters and their maintenance. In many buildings NIOSH and HBI inspectors found air supply systems completely compromised by dirty ductwork, smoke detectors

and fire dampers blocked by dirt, sealed reheat coils, turning vanes and exhaust grilles. Large quantities of bacteria and fungi were found throughout the whole systems. All of these problems easily could have been prevented by responsible design and maintenance of the HVAC system and good ventilation.

HEALTH EFFECTS OF INDOOR AIR POLLUTION

The health effects of poor indoor air are very real. In a report to legislators, the EPA stated that "a conservative estimate" of the potential economic impact of employee illness and lost of productivity attributable to indoor air pollution totals between $4.4 to $5.4 billions annually ("A dose of green...," p.56).

Additional concern is caused by the fact that the people most susceptible to the effects of air quality–children, the elderly, and the chronically ill, especially those with respiratory or cardiovascular diseases–are often the most exposed to indoor pollutants since they spend greater amounts of time indoors. A small, but growing, percentage of the population is sensitive to even very low concentrations of some chemicals often present in indoor air. This syndrome, called Multiple Chemical Sensitivities (MCS), is now recognized as a disability by the Social Security Administration and HUD. The designer's responsibility is to address the special needs of the client, which may include dangers of prolonged exposure or sensitivity to chemical substances.

In the Report to Congress on IAQ the EPA noted also that "there may be additive or synergistic effects from multiple chemical contaminants at levels below thresholds known to cause health effects. Exposure to combinations of indoor air pollutants

Side note:
A project in Lajerbo, Denmark, 1990 was devoted totally to the idea of providing low-density affordable housing for people suffering from a number of different allergies. "The object of the project was to examine the evidence for a possible reduction of environmental problems in modern tightly sealed dwellings, by the use of carefully selected building materials and increased ventilation. Each dwelling has its own ventilating system, ensuring a complete hourly air change. The system is equipped with a pollen filter. In wet rooms, the exhaust function has been increased by 10 percent. A heat-recovery system keeps the energy requirement down to a level only slightly higher than in houses with less frequent air change. Interviews with tenants have indicated much satisfaction with the indoor environment" (Holdsworth and Sealey, p.105).

may generate acute reactions in some people" (U.S. EPA, "Report...," p.3). Synergy is a term used to describe the interaction between elements (drugs, chemicals etc.) in which the combined effect exceeds the sum of their individual effects. Synergy, or "cocktail effect," as some of the researchers call it, in the indoor environment means that two, or more, air pollutants may produce higher risks for the occupants than either of them does individually. For example, the cancer risk from asbestos or radon is higher for smokers. The concept of synergy should also be applied in a broader meaning. Addressing one issue in an interior environment does not guarantee achieving a healthy interior. All of the pollutants have to be identified and controlled to the best possible degree.

General regulations for the industry are gathered by the Occupational Safety and Health Administration (OSHA). These regulations protect workers against the most extreme examples of indoor air pollution, mainly the air pollution generated in manufacturing. Theoretically, the regulations of OSHA should help protect office workers against indoor air pollution, but "the complex nature of the pollution in sick buildings and the ambiguous nature of its health effects has resulted in very little regulatory action to date" (Harte et al., p.53).

It is unfortunate, but in many cases the new spin on environmental requirements has nothing to do with growing concerns about the global situation, or peoples' health and well-being. It is simply being fueled by economics. As public awareness of indoor pollution and the health hazards caused by air contamination increases, the numbers of lawsuits related to indoor air quality has also increased. The risk of being sued starts with the employer, or owner of the building, but can end at the manufacturer and the specifier–the interior designer who, indirectly, endorses the product.

Side note:
"In a recent U.S. court case, an individual successfully sued a carpet manufacturer for injury to health caused by emissions from carpet. In a summary of the case it was noted: 'Although the legal obligations of architects and designers vis-a-vis indoor air pollution have yet to be determined, lawyers in the field recommend that they not specify any new products that have not been tested. Architects and designers should obtain pollution and toxicity information from suppliers and manufacturers and check standards with local government agencies"("Global..., p.36").

•••

Indoor air quality affects human health, safety and, in consequence human well-being and productivity. It can be improved, or degraded, by the choices the interior designers make. To control indoor air quality interior designers must become more knowledgeable about the complicated nature of buildings, systems, materials, technologies of furniture, finishes, fabrics and other interior accessories, and then use that knowledge in every decision they make.

Additional information

More in-depth analysis can be found in:

Agran, Larry. *The Cancer Connection and What We Can Do About It.* New York: St. Martin's Press, 1977

Harte, John, Cheryl Holdren, Richard Schneider, and Christine Shirley. *Toxics A to Z. A Guide to Everyday Pollution Hazards.* Berkeley and Los Angeles: University of California Press, 1991.

Holdsworth, Bill and Antony Sealey. *Healthy Buildings. A Design Primer for a Living Environment.* Essex: Longman Group UK Ltd., 1992.

United States Environmental Protection Agency (EPA). 1989. "Report to Congress on Indoor Air Quality, Vol II: Assessment and Control of Indoor Air Pollution." Washington, DC.

United States Environmental Protection Agency (EPA). 1990. "Evaluation of the Potential Carcinogenicity of Electromagnetic Fields, Draft Report." Washington, DC.

United States Environmental Protection Agency (EPA). 1991. "Building Air Quality. A Guide for Building Owners and Facility Managers." Washington, DC.

United States Environmental Protection Agency (EPA). 1991. "Introduction to Indoor Air Quality. A Reference Manual." EPA/400/3-91/003. Washington, DC.

48

Part II:
Interior Design Process

Environmentally conscious interior design can be defined as professional practice that attempts to create indoor spaces that are environmentally sustainable and healthy for the occupants. There are both direct and indirect relations between interiors and the environment: interiors generate pollution and require resources to construct and to support their functioning. The interior itself is a product, but it is also a shell, which encloses a microcosm–an unique environment with air quality as a direct, immediate effect of this shell's construction and furnishing.

Addressing all of the global environmental problems described in Part I, Environmental Issues, would bring interior design closer to the concept of sustainable architecture, which "recognizes that human civilization is an integral part of the natural world and that nature must be preserved and perpetuated if the human community is to sustain itself indefinitely. Sustainable design is the philosophy that human development should exemplify the principles of conservation, and encourage the application of those principles in our daily lives" (US Dept. of the Int., p.4). Sustainable architecture involves site sensitive building design, the use of alternative energy sources, waste control, water recycling and control of building operations and maintenance. In such a broad meaning, the idea of fully sustainable architecture lies beyond the interior designers' area of influence, unless they are working as a team in collaboration with architects, developers, engineers, environmental consultants and facility/buildings

managers. But there are still many decisions within the interior design practice itself that can and should be made to lessen the devastating impact on the global environment.

Just as achieving sustainable interiors falls within the focus of responsible designers, so the quest for a healthy indoor environment, with air free of chemicals and toxins, is very much a part of interior design professional ethics and responsibility.

Some of the design solutions described in Part II are inherent in thoughtful professional interior design practice. While providing comfort for occupants and clients, designers often can make decisions that are beneficial for the environment as well. For example: appropriate lighting design accommodates the occupants with sufficient light and, at the same time, saves energy; the appropriate choices of materials and products support responsible manufacturing processes and, simultaneously, provide a healthy indoor environment. For many practicing designers those are the obvious design choices. They may require initial conceptual effort rather then additional expense.

CHAPTER 3
RESOURCES CONSERVATION
AND POLLUTION PREVENTION

The definition of sustainable development speaks about meeting the needs of the present without compromising the ability of future generations to meet their own needs. Today's intensive exploitation of nonrenewable natural resources is one of the most immediate concerns. Until sustainable, clean technologies become everyday reality, conservation, efficiency and recycling are the most economical and the only rational way of insuring a sustainable future.

Interior designers can have an impact on natural resources conservation and lowering outdoor pollution through energy conservation and energy efficiency; through water conservation; and through promotion of recycling, use of recycled and recyclable materials and products.

ENERGY EFFICIENCY AND CONSERVATION

According to the analysis undertaken by Croxton Collaborative and physicist Francesco Tubiello, 54 percent of the primary energy in the United States is consumed by the built environment. "The built environment is thus the major user of energy; by the same token, building professionals have the opportunity to contribute significantly to overall energy conservation" (*Audubon House*, p. 26). In the future, use of renewable energy resources, such as sun, wind, geothermal and biogas conversion, may change the situation, but until then, designers are responsible for limiting devastating effects of today's power generation methods through designing for energy efficiency and conservation.

Energy conservation in buildings is an enormous and very complex issue. It involves construction methods, use and control of daylight, choices of finishes and colors, decisions made in design of artificial lighting, selection of HVAC systems and other equipments. The amount of energy required for the building is determined as much by the proper design concept, focused on energy conservation, as by the specification of particular energy efficient lighting and equipment.

Energy efficient lighting

"Lighting accounts for a large percentage of the energy dollar spent to operate the office. In most instances it amounts to approximately 33 percent. In some cases it totals more than 60 percent. Lighting–commercial, industrial, and residential–consumes a substantial portion of the electrical energy generated in this nation. Anything that can be done to reduce this portion is beneficial to the nation as a whole, as well as to the overhead of individual offices."
(Cohen and Cohen, p.187).

Wrongly applied, too much or too little, lighting can have a negative effect on productivity, the mood and comfort of the people, and the aesthetic impact of an interior. Depending on its character and function, lighting design for a space has to provide appropriate conditions for various activities performed. Building codes include energy budget requirements for lighting that are based on a particular type of space use. Knowing what the available choices are is vital for making educated decisions. The designer's goal is to provide comfort, to satisfy aesthetic requirements and, at the same time, to limit the use of energy and lower the cost of maintenance.

• Use of natural light

Well controlled natural light, supported by light-dispersing and light-reflecting materials, can provide good, healthy and inexpensive illumination. The very first step in deciding about lighting design for the interior should be a study of the natural light conditions, which includes an analysis of climate, site, fenestration, externally and internally reflected light, and the occupants' needs.

The more natural light that is provided and the deeper it penetrates into the interior, the less electric light will be needed and the less energy will be consumed. The easiest way to allow more daylight into a space would be to use very large openings–clear glass widows, clerestories, or skylights–with a minimum of controls. But direct sunshine and a direct view of the sky can expose occupants to excessive contrast in brightness, resulting in poor visibility and discomfort. To prevent the negative effects of natural light, shading and control devices are used to reflect the sun but admit the daylight.

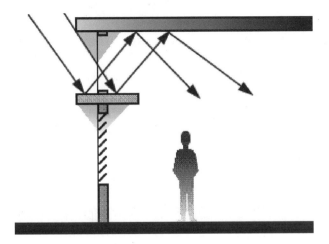

Fig. II-1:
Bringing in daylight through openings located on the top of a wall allow reflected light to penetrate even deeper into the interior space.

One of the most effective ways of controlling daylight is the use of reflected light. Each time daylight is reflected from a surface, it is spread and softened. Reflecting daylight reduces light intensity and eliminates contrast by evening the general brightness patterns, in effect, increasing visibility and improving quality of light in the interior. The harshness of direct sunlight can be additionally filtered before it enters the interior by outside trees, shrubs, vines, curtains, reflective "shelves," or louvers.

There are varieties of interior louvers for daylight control. One of the most effective are venetian blinds; they can be adjusted each time the conditions outside change or the inside needs vary. Venetian blinds can exclude direct sunshine but reflect the light to the ceiling where it will bounce into the interior (Fig. II-2). Tilted to the closed position blinds will essentially block all daylight and view. One of the innovations was developed in Europe, slender blinds installed between two window panels. Enclosure eliminates the dirt-collection problem and the clumsiness of the control strings.

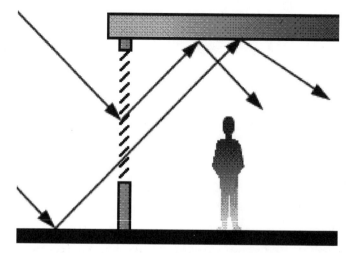

Fig. II-2:
Venetian blinds take advantage of reflected ground light by bouncing it deep into the interior of the space

Horizontal louvers are the most effective on southern exposure windows (Fig. II-3); vertical louvers are suitable for low sun angles on windows facing east or west (Fig. II-4). For situations where both the high and low sun must be considered, egg-crate louvers are the most effective control, since they combine the characteristics of both horizontal and vertical louvers. The egg-crate louvers block the direct sun rays but reflect daylight into the space. Since they prevent a view of the bright sky from the interior, egg-crate louvers are the most effective when used on the upper part of the window.

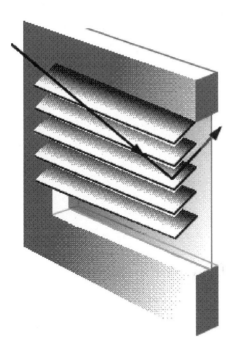

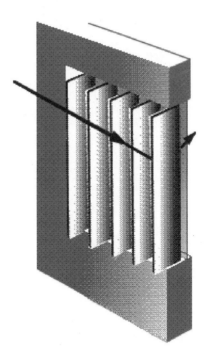

Fig. II-3:
Horizontal louvers are effective when the sun is high in the sky (south-facing wall).

Fig. II-4:
Vertical louvers are effective when the sun is low in the sky (west-facing wall).

Side note:
"[Tinted glazing materials] are produced principally in gray and bronze, or variations thereof, although they are available in other colors. The gray materials are neutral so that interior colors are rendered realistically, but colored transparent materials will distort the appearance of interior colors and should be avoided. Light transmittances of these tinted materials range from the very dark (10 to 15 percent) to very light (70 to 80 percent) and their transmittance of the infrared spectrum (heat producing) is only slightly more restricted–usually 10 to 15 percent below that of the visible transmittance." (Evans, p.89).

Side note:
Ultraviolet radiation, which in case of overexposure can cause damage to the skin, or even malignant tumors, supplied in proper amount has all the beneficial effects. It produces vitamin D and keeps the skin in a healthy condition. "When the body is exposed to ultraviolet rays there is a dilation of the capillaries of the skin. Blood pressure falls slightly. In addition to a feeling of well-being, there is a quickening of the pulse rate and appetite, plus a stimulation of energetic activity. Work output may actually be increased" (Evans, p.20). In the artificial environment we receive almost no health-giving ultraviolet. Incandescent and fluorescent light is almost completely lacking in ultraviolet. Some of the new light sources include ultraviolet in their output.

Draperies are another way to control sunlight. Depending on the weave and reflectivity of the fabric, they can provide a complete blackout or just about any degree of light transmission desired. More flexibility can be achieved through the use of two separately tracked draperies over the same opening.

The light entering the interior can be also controlled through the selection of glazing material. Selectively transmitting materials permit the passage of some parts of the radiant energy spectrum, while reflecting or absorbing others. Widely used selectively transmitting materials are tinted glasses and plastics. The negative aspect of their performance is that they affect perception of the light outside the window. Glazing materials treated with metallic or metallic oxide coatings or films, which reflect light rather than transmit or absorb it, reduce the view into the interior from outside during the day. In the evening hours, however, they produce the undesirable opposite effect, putting the interior "on display," while not letting the occupants see outside.

Design that utilizes daylight as a important component must be integrated with other environmental concerns: view, natural air movement, acoustics, heat gain and loss and electric lighting. For example, an operable window will allow daylight and natural air flow, but it will also allow noise to enter the space.

In making appropriate decisions about daylight, the designer needs to address more than just the cost of energy. It has been proven that the full spectrum of light, the main characteristic of daylight, is one of the biological needs of all living organisms, including people. People need to relate to natural surroundings both mentally and physically. In interiors completely deprived of natural light people often lose track of time, do not know outside weather

conditions, and feel disoriented.

• Lighting system design

A well thought through lighting design takes into consideration the principal needs of the occupants and encourages the use of as much light as is needed at a particular moment. A thorough study of the interior's daylighting conditions and the tasks performed at various time of the day dictates any further decisions of supplementing daylight with artificial lighting. The first requirement is to provide the appropriate quantity of light, that is, the amount of light necessary to perform specific tasks within a given area. The general rule to be applied is that activities of greater visual difficulty require higher illumination. Thus, corridors do not need to be lit as brightly as a reading room. The age of the occupants (an average 60-year-old person needs a light level 10 percent higher than that of a 20-year-old) and the aesthetics of the space are additional elements to be considered when designing lighting systems. Energy conservation guidelines for New York State call for electric lighting systems to operate at a maximum power density of 2.4 watts per square foot. Not only can this be achieved, it has often been lowered with carefully designed lighting systems.

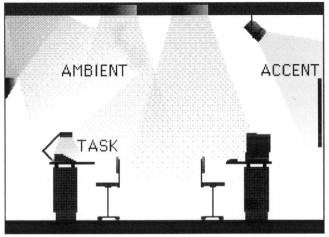

AMBIENT   ACCENT

TASK

Fig. II-5:
It is a good practice to define
three major kinds of lighting: ambient,
accent and task, and to provide
separate circuiting for each of them.

Side note:
The Croxton Collaborative, in their "state of the environmental art" project–the Audubon Society headquarters building in New York–installed motion sensors that detect whether someone is in a room; after a specified number of minutes without movement, the lights are switched off until someone enters the room again. "Using these sensors, Mr. Croxton said, leads to an immediate 30 percent reduction in consumption. An added benefit is that there is a reduced lighting-produced heat load" (Mead, p.15).

A comfortable light level with appropriate power density can be easily satisfied by defining light zones and providing a variety of ambient, accent and task lighting. Separate circuiting and switching should be supplied for each zone, and for each task light. The initial expense of extra switches and extra yards of cable will be quickly returned in savings on energy costs. A continuously fully lit interior is not only unpleasant, it is also a waste of energy.

By providing a variety of independent task lights in interiors, the designer can achieve the most important goal: good illumination where it is needed and no waste of energy where it is unnecessary. Light from overhead sources causes shadows cast by a person's head and can cause glare on work surfaces ("veiling reflection"). Task lighting places the light directly at the task and allows for control over the lighting angle, while reducing the requirements for constant ambient light levels. The best task light comes between the head of a person working and his/her work surface, is uniformly distributed, and does not cause glare. This can be achieved through use of recessed or track-mounted lighting, pendants, properly spaced miniature track lights and spots, desk light fixtures or tubular lamps tucked under cabinets or shelves. Task lighting should also relate to the visual difficulty of the activity performed, which is determined by three elements: size of objects viewed, contrast between objects and background, and luminance of objects.

To ensure benefits from proper zoning and circuiting, convenient, easily accessible light controls have to be provided so that all the possible combinations will be used. It is important, for example, to analyze traffic in the spaces and provide on/off switches at every entrance. Occupancy sensors, dimming, stepped switching and programmable timing controls are, in addition to energy efficient lamps, recognized for energy credits from utility companies.

When considering the lighting costs of an installation, it is important to address both the initial cost (cost of the lighting components plus the labor costs of installation) and the operating costs (the energy consumption and maintenance costs).

• Lamps

Available energy efficient lamps provide a wide variety of colors and light renditions. There is no longer any excuse for specifying the least efficient incandescent lamps. The possible additional initial cost of halogen, fluorescent or high intensity discharge lamps is quickly returned in the savings on the cost of energy, prolonged lifespan of the lamp, and lower cost of maintenance. The environmental benefit is immediate in lowering energy demand. When considering lamps for hard-to-reach fixtures, it is important to look for a kind that combines energy savings with long life, since this will limit maintenance cost and will lower demand for replacement.

-Incandescent lighting

Incandescent lamps are known for their lack of efficiency: up to 90 percent of the electric energy in incandescent lighting is lost to heat; only 10 percent is used to produce light. In addition the heat generated by this type of lamp increases the need for cooling the interior in the warm season. Another drawback is the short life, which for standard incandescent lamps is just 750 hours. If the use of incandescent light is unavoidable there are some simple rules that can help limiting use of energy:

> • Use one large lamp rather than several smaller ones; this will produce more overall light. In other words, one 100-watt incandescent bulb gives

Side note:
"No bulb is cheaper to buy and more expensive to use than an incandescent bulb" (US Dept. of Int., p.72).

more light than three 40-watt bulbs, while using 20 watts less electricity;

• Use three-way lamps where possible and switch to a lower wattage when bright light is not needed;

• Use dimmers, which adds to the flexibility of light load;

• Use energy-saving incandescent lamps, which in most cases can replace standard lamps without visible difference: a 40-watt lamp can be replaced by a 34-watt lamp; 60-watt by 52-watt, 75-watt by 67-watt, and so on.

-Halogen lamps

Halogen lamps are an efficient form of incandescent lighting that can provide energy savings along with the optical characteristics necessary for point source illumination. The lamps contains halogen gas to produce brighter, whiter light. The inert halogen gas also prolongs the life of the lamp. They are available in either standard or low-voltage designs. Standard lamps are approximately 20 percent more efficient than standard incandescent. Low-voltage halogen reflector lamps have many advantages compared with standard incandescent, including: a 40 percent higher energy efficiency achieved through increased efficacy (the rate at which a lamp is able to convert electrical power (watts) into light (lumens), expressed in terms of lumens per watt (LPW)), lightweight compact light source, 2000 hour life span, and much better light output as they age. Halogen lamps with their integral reflectors provide a choice of high intensity beams suitable for professional spotlighting, task lighting and for accent lighting.

-Fluorescent lighting.

"The moment someone mentions using fluorescent, your eyes glaze and you slowly start backing away with your arms crossed over your face" (Whitehead, p.15). This kind of a reaction should be a thing of the past. Recently huge improvements have been made in fluorescent technology. There are now more than 220 colors from which to choose (incandescent light is always one color). For example, trichromatic phosphor fluorescent lamps combine all three of the primary colors–green, blue and red–and produce a highly efficient white light which, by changing the proportions of the primary colors, can be made cooler or warmer. The compact fluorescent, designed to replace incandescent lamps in task and downlighting, solved the problem of size and design of lighting fixtures. Today's high-frequency electronic ballasts not only start the lamps instantly but also eliminate the flicker and hum, which for many were the main problems of fluorescent lamps.

The benefits are great: fluorescent lamps give three to five times more light (60 lumens per watt) from the same amount of energy than conventional incandescent (15 lumens per watt), and they can last

Replacing one A-line incandescent with compact fluorescent saves:
• 45W
• 157.5 kWh/yr.
It also prevents release to the atmosphere:
• 300 lbs CO_2/yr
• 1.4 lbs SO_2/yr
• 0.8 lbs NO_x/yr.

A-line incandescent

Compact fluorescent

Fig. II-6:
Energy savings per socket

(source: Dana, "An Ounce...," p.111)

Side note:
Improved color high pressure sodium sources produce a white light comparable to incandescent. They have an outstanding color rendering index of 80, a color temperature of 2700K, and 10,000-hour life. These lamps are also highly energy efficient: a 50-watt lamp provides more lumens than a 100-watt incandescent. In addition, because of candlepower distribution, they can be used as accent, display, wallwashing or downlights.
"White SON [example of such a high pressure sodium lamp] provides warm, crisp light, like sunshine on a clear day, in contrast to the 'cloudy-day' light from some fluorescent lighting and the cool color of metal halide," says Gary Gordon of Gary Gordon Architectural Lighting, New York ("White SON...," p.1).

up to 22,000 hours. They will lower every month's utility bill and significantly decrease demand for replacement. Using fluorescent light also helps to reduce the use of energy for air conditioning by reducing the amount of heat emitted. Exchanging just one incandescent lamp with a compact fluorescent will keep a half-ton of carbon dioxide out of the atmosphere over the life of that lamp. "If every household in the United States replaced one incandescent light bulb with a fluorescent, the reduction in air emissions would be equal to three major power plants" ("A healthy...," p.2).

-High intensity discharge lamps

High intensity discharge lamps (HIDs) have become increasingly important in recent years. They have even higher efficiency than fluorescent lighting and a life span of up to 24,000 hours. For a long time their use was limited to outdoor or industrial applications because their color properties were inadequate for interiors, but now, with over 60 varied colors, HIDs have begun to replace fluorescent and incandescent lamps in indoor applications.

The three main types of HID lamps are named for the different materials contained in the lamp's arc tube. The material affects the lamp light coloring. Mercury lamps generate more wavelengths in the blue-green range of the spectrum. High pressure sodium lamps highlight the red-yellow range. New versions offer warm, incandescent-like color and are particularly suitable for retail application. Metal halide lamps render the most natural light and are being used more and more in lighting stores and public spaces.

In addition, in all the lamps described above the overall efficiency is also influenced by the design of the fixture, the age of a lamp, and the regularity of cleaning.

• **Colors and finishes**

The quality of light can be easily changed by altering the colors and reflectance of all surfaces in an interior: walls, ceiling, floor finish or covering, and furnishings. It is basic knowledge that dark colors

SURFACE	%
White-painted wallboard	
new	75–90
old	50–70
White plaster	90–92
Brick	
light buff	40–45
red	10–20
Wood	
light birch	35–50
light oak	25–35
walnut	5–10

Fig. II-7:
Approximate reflectance of surfaces.

COLOR	%
White	*80
Ivory (light)	71
Apricot beige	66
Lemon yellow	65
Ivory (dark)	59
Light buff	56
Peach	53
Salmon	53
Pale apple green	51
Pale blue	51
Medium gray	43
Light green	41
Deep rose	12
Dark green	9
Black	*1

Fig. II-8:
Approximate reflectance of paints.

"Technically black and white are not colors. Pure black absorbs 100 percent of the light, while pure white reflects it. In the office environment pure black and white are impossible to achieve. Furthermore, surface textures and finishes modify reflectance. A glossy finish is more reflectant than a matte finish. A buildup of dirt and grime also modifies reflectance. Glossy finishes tend to stay cleaner than matte finishes, but tend to produce glare".

(Cohen and Cohen, p.208)

absorb light and pale colors reflect it. The use of paler hues and tones on walls and ceilings increases the usable light. For small spaces it is always advisable to use lighter colors of finishes. Raising the average reflectance of the space will brighten the room, but when planning the use of glossy finishes designers have to be careful to avoid glare.

Electrical equipment and appliances

In 1987, the US Congress, over the objections of the Department of Energy, but with the backing of utilities, appliance manufacturers, and environmental groups, passed the National Appliance Energy Conservation Act. This law sets minimum efficiency criteria for HVAC systems, refrigerators, freezers, and other appliances.

Room Air Conditioner
Capacity: 6,000 BTU/hr

ENERGYGUIDE

Models with the most efficient energy rating number use less energy and cost less to operate.

Models with 5,800 to 6,299 BTU's cool about the same space.

Least efficient model
6.6

9.5

Most efficient model
9.5

THIS MODEL ▼

Energy Efficiency Rating (EER)

Your cost will vary depending on your local energy rate and how you use the product. This energy cost is based on U.S. Government standard tests.
How much will this model cost you to run yearly?

Yearly hours of use		250	750	1000	2000	3000
		Estimated yearly $ cost shown below				
Cost per kilowatt hour	2¢	$3	$9	$13	$25	$38
	4¢	$6	$19	$25	$51	$76
	6¢	$9	$28	$38	$76	$114
	8¢	$13	$38	$51	$101	$152
	10¢	$16	$47	$63	$126	$189
	12¢	$19	$57	$76	$152	$227

Ask your salesperson or local utility for the energy rate (cost per kilowatt hour) in your area. Your cost will vary depending on your local energy rate and how you use the product.

Important Removal of this label before consumer purchase is a violation of federal law (42 U.S.C. 6302)

1165637

Fig. II-9:
Example of Energy Efficiency Rating on a room air conditioner EnergyGuide label.

When specifying any electrical equipment or appliances, it is very important to look for the Energy Efficiency Rating (EER) and the estimated yearly operating cost. These are listed on the yellow-and-black federal EnergyGuide label attached to every air conditioner, fan, dishwasher, dryer, refrigerator, freezer, and so on.

It is also important to determine what equipment is the most effective for any particular function, for example, providing window fans can effectively cool an interior for many of the warm days and they can be less costly to operate than an air conditioner.

For some appliances, the use of a timer, thermostat or a sensor can save energy, without decreasing the comfort of the occupants. A photocell can control day and night operation. An air conditioner timer can be set to turn the unit on or off depending on the peoples' presence in the space, outside temperature changes, or based on a preprogrammed time schedule.

Sophisticated and sensitive electronic equipment is progressively becoming a greater part of commercial building electrical loads. This equipment includes computers, building automation systems, telephone automation systems, printers, fax machines, electronic ballasts, PC networks and copiers. All these developments can be considered energy-conserving, since they limit space requirements, reduce the need for direct meetings, replace hand delivery of documents, and so on.

Climate control

The responsible design and choice of an HVAC system is particularly crucial in establishing the building's indoor air quality and use of energy. Recent increases in ASHRAE ventilation requirements, including increased minimum air exchange rate, if applied without any other

Side note:
Important information for the residential and commercial clients is that an average refrigerator made today uses only half the energy of one made in 1973. That means a quick payback for the up-front investment in a newer model. Switching from an old refrigerator to a new one saves 1000 kilowatt hours per year, eliminating 1.35 lb of nitrous oxide and .37 lb of sulfur dioxide from the environment.

(Source: "Cold Facts...," pp. 7-9)

improvements in the design of the ventilation system, result in increased energy consumption. A recent study "Found increases in energy use ranging from less then one percent to about eight percent for heating, and less then one to almost fourteen percent for cooling.... The maximum percentage increase in operating cost for all locations examined is less than five percent" (Gordon, p. 45). The increases in energy requirements can be offset or even eliminated through improvements in the building's insulation, lighting design, HVAC, and other equipment efficiency. The solutions range from heat reclamation, thermal-storage systems, flexible air-handling and chiller units, to building designs which allow natural ventilation. Decisions regarding buildings systems usually fall into the domain of architects or, even more, the engineers, but responsibility for finding appropriate solutions depends on creativity and integrated efforts in which interior designers should play a significant role.

One of the most direct ways interior designers can control the indoor climate is through the choices of window frames and glazing materials. Windows and skylights typically account for up to 25 percent of a building's energy loss. Aluminum frames without

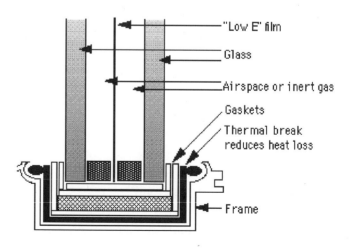

Fig. II-10:
High performance window: the "low E" film reduces heating and cooling loads with little effect on visible light.

thermal breaks are very inefficient. All outside windows produced today have two layers of glass, but their energy efficiency can be improved with low-E coatings. "E" stands for emission and refers to a window's ability to absorb or reflect radiant energy. "Low E" windows cost only 10-15 percent more than traditional double panel units, but reduce the energy loss up to 18 percent. Another way of increasing the insulating qualities of windows is by filling the space between the panes with argon or krypton gas. Appropriate windows can reduce the cost of heating/ventilating by minimizing the influence of outside temperature and sunlight. They can also reduce maintenance, noise and condensation problems; the initial cost will usually pay for itself.

Characteristics of high performance windows include:

- Double or triple gasketed opening sashes;
- "Thermal break" design (for metal sash);
- Double or triple sealed panes filled with inert gas;
- A "low E" coating to reduce heat transfer.

The National Fenestration Rating Council, established in 1992, developed a procedure that consists of a variety of simulations and tests to determine accurately the U-value of fenestration products. "U" is the unit expressing "heat flow through a building section including air spaces 3/4 inch or greater and air films. Technically, it is heat transmission in Btu's per hour per square foot per degree F difference from air to air" (Ramsey and Sleeper, p. 318). Once the testing and evaluation of windows has been completed by one of the independent laboratories, the manufacturer is authorized to label their products. The label identifies the product and shows its U-value. This system gives

Side note:
Windows, Daylighting Group at Lawrence Berkeley Laboratory in Berkeley, California, developed an IBM-compatible computer program for calculating window thermal performance. The program is consistent with NFRC rating procedures and, as it is in the public domain can be obtained free of charge from the NFRC at 962 Wayne Avenue, Suite 750, Silver Spring, MD, or Bostik Construction Products, P.O. Box 8, Huntington Valley, PA 19006.

Side note:
In-Sol Drapes, a combination of mylar and polished aluminum, designed by Frank Bateman, the Massachusetts-based designer, stop as much as 80 percent of heat loss through windows. The reflecting material also keeps out destructive ultraviolet rays of the sun. Any fabric can be added to the drapery material for aesthetic purposes ("Environmentally Concerned...", p.19).

designers, engineers and architects the capability of evaluating the energy properties of windows and makes heat gain/loss calculation more reliable.

The cooling and heating demands of buildings are also affected by window treatments. Draperies or blinds can cut down on, or allow for air and sunlight penetration. The choice of window treatments should acknowledge the climate outside and the sun exposure of the interior. Outside controls–awnings, overhangs, louvers, trees or overhanging plants–are also effective in limiting influences of the weather conditions

• • •

It is appropriate to remind the reader that saving energy is an alternative to generating more energy and building new power plants. The benefits of energy efficiency and conservation are:
- Lower operating costs, resulting from lower energy and maintenance cost;
- Reduced demand on power generation, resulting in less air and water pollution, and decreased consumption of nonrenewable energy resources.

WATER CONSERVATION

Side note:
Each person in the USA produces almost 20,000 gallons of sewage a year (Lyle, p. 225).

The extent of water contamination is enormous. This situation cannot discourage the desire to change; on the contrary, it should fuel the need for immediate action. The most polluting industries (i.e., steel, paper and textile industries) have to be monitored and products whose manufacturing includes highly toxic technologies should be avoided. In residential, institutional and commercial design, water conservation should be promoted through specifications of water conserving appliances and through water recycling systems that limit demand and decrease sewage.

The cost of installing low-flow faucets and shower heads can pay back not only in water conservation and lower water bills, but also in energy savings. Water conservation goes together with energy efficiency, especially whenever use of hot water is considered. Four percent of the US national energy use is for domestic water heating (after: Brown et al., p.195). With every extra minute spent in the shower, the hot water puts 1/2 lb of carbon dioxide into the air. One of the techniques of energy conservation is eliminating heat loss through heat tracing on hot-water pipes, or heating water with solar energy. Water conservation can be also improved by recycling potable water and secondary reuse such as waste-water to flush toilets.

In residential buildings, the main demand for water is caused by toilets. Their wasteful construction not only depletes a great portion of drinking water, but also adds to sewage problems. A new law, effective in 1992, mandates installation of low-flow toilets (using 1.6 gallons a flush) in new construction and in major renovation projects.

Side note:
New York City's estimated 4 million toilets use up to eight gallons a flush and accounts alone for as much as 40 percent of the total household water consumption. The Plumbing Foundation and two New York City agencies conducted a pilot program that showed that installation of low-flow toilets in 20-unit buildings lowered water consumption by approximately 30 to 40 percent over similar size buildings with traditional plumbing (Goldstein and Izeman, p.145).

Fig. II-11:
Low-flow toilets use 1.6 gallons of water per flush instead of typical 3.5.
(Photo: courtesy of American Standard, Inc.)

Side note:
• Low-flow aerators installed on faucets can save up to 50 percent of water.

• Low-flow shower heads use up to 70 percent less water than standard shower heads.

• Toilet dams installed in toilet tanks limit the amount of water per flush.

An holistic design of sustainable building would include the use of rainwater, switching to non-potable sources–"gray water"–for some uses, or composting organic kitchen and toilets waste. The technologies are already available and it is the collective responsibility of architects, engineers and interior designers to promote their use. William McDonough, a New York based architect, one of the pioneers of "green" architecture, included recycling technology of "grey and black" water in his design for Eurosud-Calvisson, a software research development facility and university in southern France (Wagner, "Visionary...," p.56).

Today, specifying water-conserving faucets, and low-flow toilets is a basic part of responsible interior design practice.

CONSERVATION OF OTHER RESOURCES

Waste management

Every product, piece of equipment, material, finish, and so on, in every building and interior represents certain amounts of natural resources–renewable or nonrenewable–used to create, process and maintain it, and the energy needed for excavation, cultivation, transportation, manufacturing, processing, shaping, treating, and so on. A variety of materials and energy is being used at every step. The best possible way of insuring a sustainable future is through recycling the resources and energy once invested in processed products. Reuse, recycling, use of recycled and recyclable materials guarantee sustainable resources management, limit pollution and are the only sensible answer to the solid waste problem.

John Tillman Lyle in *Regenerative Design for Sustainable Development* suggests that: "Much of our difficulty with waste is embedded in the word itself. Waste is defined as material considered worthless and thrown away after use. In this sense it is a human invention, essential to the one-way flows of the throughput system; this definition depends on the assumption that energy and materials, having once served our immediate purposes, can simply cease to exist in any functional sense." None of the mainstream disposal systems (landfilling, incineration, sewage treatments) recognizes waste as a resource. To change the accelerating consumption of natural resources, and to limit pollution, it is necessary to replace the dominating "one way" linear model by the 'cyclical' model in which waste will cease to exist.

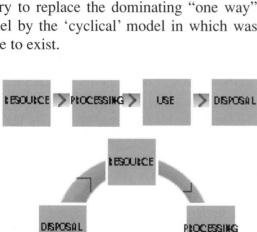

Fig. II-12:
Linear and cyclical models.

Any of the traditional "disposal" systems can be designed in such a way as to became a source for energy, or storage for the future when the technology will be available for reuse. Proper design may also speed up decomposition of organic parts of the refuse

Side note:

The question is: How can we avoid being buried in our own refuse? The obvious answer is by source reduction, that is, by creating less waste in the first place.

- The more potential waste we reuse, the less there is to get rid of.
- Recycling conserves natural resources and energy, limits pollution, and saves money.

Side note:

Herman Miller, furniture manufacturer, reduced 95 percent of their landfill space through the generating of heat energy for steam and air conditioning from their wood products scrap.

and make them available as fertilizer. Some of the technologies are already available, but until they are introduced into the mainstream, the focus has to be on recycling and limiting waste.

Since waste from construction and demolition is one of the biggest contributors to landfills, when it is unavoidable to tear down a building or demolish an interior it is a good idea to first find out what can be recycled or salvaged. For example, gypsum board scrap is an environmental hazard that many landfills will not accept because it produces toxic hydrogen sulfide gas when buried. The same gypsum waste can be recycled with an average of about 85 percent of material reused for new gypsum boards.

In designing and constructing new spaces, it is good to keep in mind the basic categories into which the potential waste can be divided, before sending it all off to the landfill:

- Reusables–items that are no longer needed by one person (or group of people), but can be used by others, such as furniture, equipment, appliances;
- Recyclables–items that cannot be reused as is, but contain recyclable materials, such as newspapers, office paper, aluminum cans, glass, some plastics;
- Compostables–material that can be composted into nutrient-rich soil and fertilizer, such as food waste, leaves, grass clippings, and so on;
- True waste–materials that cannot be reused, recycled or composted.

Recycling cannot be accomplished without physical accommodations. Increasingly, it is up to the interior designer to locate and design a whole series of multiple bins and the trails that connect them. Often this aspect of design needs to be coordinated with material sources (such as paper suppliers) and with destinations (recycling contractors).

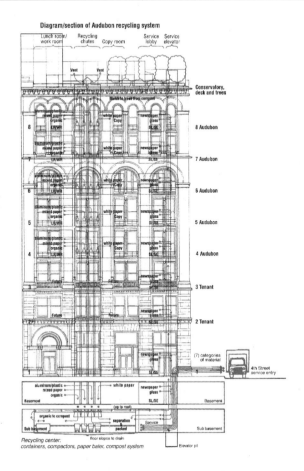

Diagram/section of Audubon recycling system

Fig. II-13:
Audubon House, elevation showing recycling system. (Courtesy of Croxton Collaborative, Architects.)

In the National Audubon Society's new headquarters in New York, designed by the Croxton Collaborative Architects, which became a laboratory and a showcase for many environmental ideas, each floor has four chutes that drop to the recycling center in the sub-basement. Each chute leads to a bin for recyclables – plastics and aluminum, food waste, and white and mixed paper. Waste is processed and packaged for transport in the basement. Cans and plastic bottles are crushed; newspaper and cardboard are bound; hazardous waste is securely enclosed for pickup; and food and other biodegradable waste is composted and used in potted plants throughout the building and in a terrace garden on the roof. The goal is to recycle 80 percent of everything that comes into the building.

In this project, the renovation of the existing building, recycling and reusing materials from interior demolition was done with both environment and cost in mind. The renovation of the existing structure, itself, saved the energy otherwise required to tear down a building and to construct something in its place. " It preserved in place 300 tons of steel, 9,000 tons of masonry and 560 tons of concrete" (Mead, p.15).

It is important to remember that responsible resource management involves not only recycling and use of recyclable materials, but also use of products made, themselves, out of recycled materials.

Sustainable forestry

By definition, wood belongs to renewable resources, but due to thoughtless, destructive timbering and agricultural practices many species of trees are on the verge of extinction, and numerous, previously balanced, regional ecosystems have collapsed. Despite an alarming situation and the efforts on the part of environmental groups, the impact of recent protective initiatives is yet to be seen.

There is no easy way for the individual to find the "smart wood," to identify the good wood from the bad, or to distinguish well managed forests from ill-managed. To help architects and designers in specifying wood products there are certification and labeling programs for sustainably produced timber, but the process is very complicated and has only recently begun. Sustainable forest management recognizes a forest as an ecosystem within which many forces interact, including biodiversity of flora and fauna, nutrient holding capacity and regeneration of timber and nontimber species. Sustainable management is based on techniques that foster the natural regeneration of seedlings, saplings, or both, and logging operations that minimize soil erosion, and prevent damage to all forest vegetation. The sustainable management approach also requires recognition of the basic land-use rights of local indigenous populations to minimize disruption of their traditional way of life. The concept of sustained yield is still, in most cases, in the sphere of futuristic vision bordering on abstraction–only less than one-eighth of one percent of tropical logging is conducted on a sustainable basis.

Dealing responsibly with this complex issue is not an easy task. Discussion has led to a great deal of disagreement within the scientific and environmental communities, and created confusion and frustration among designers trying to make proper choices.

What designers can do at this point is to educate themselves as the specifiers and consumers, and then ask the right questions: Where did this wood come from? What kind of wood is it? What information do you as a retailer or producer have about the management of the forest this wood is derived from? The ideal answer from suppliers is that the wood comes from a forest or plantation that demonstrates a verifiable commitment to replanting and harvesting, that does not harm the old forest, and that gives new trees time to grow.

The CFC issue in interior design

Ozone depletion, which is mainly caused by CFC emissions, is one of the environmental threats that has galvanized the international community into formulating a uniform prevention policy. Now the challenge to industry is to make the transition from CFCs to substitute chemicals. CFCs in building industry found their use in refrigeration and in insulation. The rules to apply are:
- CFC-free refrigerator and air conditioning equipment;
- CFC-free insulation;
- Recovering CFCs from HVAC units that are being replaced.

Start at your own office

Responsibility for global warming, ozone depletion, devastation of forests, pollution, shrinking

natural resources, and other elements of environmental implosion always seems to lie far away. The fact is that everybody contributes to the alarming situation. For example, the average office worker in USA may discard as much as 180 pounds of high quality, recyclable paper every year. Thirty percent of the nation's energy is consumed by the building industry alone.

It would be easier to convince clients of the need for environmentally conscious design practice, and then to meet those requirements, if designers would make those practices their own. There are many environmentally responsible alternatives to wasteful daily practices, including reduction of waste through use of ceramic mugs instead of styrofoam cups, and use of double-sided copiers instead of single-sided.

William McDonough Architects, Milton Glazer, Herbert Construction, Herman Miller, the AIA, and the Interior Design Center in New York (IDCNY) prepared a permanent display at IDCNY's World Environmental Business (WEB) Center that demonstrates many of these alternatives. "The exhibit employs a mirror-image approach to contrast unconsidered office practices with benign alternatives. Red carpeting and walls cover one side of the room, denoting the typical office, while green floors and walls indicate the environmentally conscious space" (Dana, "Greening up," p.80).

Additional information

More in depth analysis can be found in:

• General:
Audubon House: Building the Environmentally Responsible, Energy-Efficient Office. National Audubon Society, Croxton Collaborative, Architects. New York: John Wiley & Sons, Inc., 1994.

Building Connections. A Three-Part Series for Architects and Allied Professionals on Design for the Environment. January 14, March 4, and April 22. Resource Supplement for Program II: Healthy Buildings and Materials. March 4, 1993. AIA. Washington, DC. 1993.

Cohen, Elaine and Aaron Cohen. *Planning the Electronic Office.* New York: McGraw-Hill Book Company, 1983.

Goldstein, Eric A. and Mark A. Izeman. *The New York Environment Book.* Natural Resources Defense Council. Washington, DC: Islan Press, 1990.

Lyle, John Tillman. *Regenerative Design for Sustainable Development.* New York: John Wiley & Sons, Inc., 1994.

• Energy efficiency including daylighting:

Evans, Benjamin, H., AIA. *Daylight in Architecture.* New York: Architectural Record Books. McGraw-Hill Book Company, 1981.

Moore, Fuller. *Concepts and Practice of Architectural Daylighting.* New York: Van Nostrand Reinhold Co., Inc., 1985.

Olgyay, Victor. *Design with Climate: Bioclimatic Approach to Architectural Regionalism.* Princeton: Princeton University Press, 1963.

CHAPTER 4
INDOOR AIR QUALITY (IAQ)

As discussed in Chapter 2, the quality of indoor air affects human health and safety and, in consequence, human well-being and productivity. The quality of indoor air can only be addressed by an holistic approach that includes building design, source of pollution control, ventilation, maintenance and monitoring. To provide occupants with healthy interiors the team of architect, engineer and interior designer has to work together. Interior designers can have an especially decided impact on sources of pollution control by specifying appropriate materials, products and equipment. To some degree designers help decide about effectively functioning ventilation, through a thoughtful study of interior space design. It is also crucial that interior designers provide building's management, users and owners with sufficient information about maintenance requirements.

The main sources of indoor air pollution can be grouped into three categories:
- Indoor materials, finishes, furnishings and equipment;
- Chemicals used within the building; and
- Human activities and biological processes.

Since human activities and biological processes will always build up a certain amount of indoor pollution, the goal is to reduce the other sources and to provide for sufficient air purification and exchange.

SOURCE OF POLLUTION CONTROL

The most effective way of limiting indoor air pollution is through the control of pollution sources. Some of the criteria that should be applied while selecting all materials, products and equipment for

a healthy indoor environment include:
- Emissions–compounds that are likely to be emitted into the air from the material or product during installation and use;
- Toxicity–emitted compounds that are health hazards;
- Exposure–surface of the material exposed to indoor air and to people; and
- Maintenance requirements–cleaning, stain resistance treatment, waxing and other high impact maintenance requirements of the material or product.

(Based on: "Global choices...," p.42.)

By law, manufacturers of products that may have health and safety implications are required to provide a summary of the chemical composition of the material, including health risks, flammability, handling and storage precautions, and so on. The information is gathered on the Manufacturers Safety Data Sheets (MSDS). Some of the terms used in MSDSs include:
- Threshold Limit Value (TLV)–the accepted toxicity threshold for a hazardous material–the lower the TLV, the more toxic the agent is;
- Time Weighted Average (TWA)–the allowable exposure limit over a working day–the lower the TWA, the more toxic the agent is;
- Lethal Dose, 50 percent (LD50)–the dose expressed in milligrams per kg of body weight which is lethal to 50 percent of laboratory animals when ingested–the lower the LD50, the more toxic the agent is;
- Total Volatile Organic Content (TVOC)–the volume of the product that will evaporate over time–the higher the TVOC the more the product adds to indoor pollution.

(After: "Global choices...," p.43.)

It is advisable to request the MSDS information for all products and materials used indoors. For materials and products with questionable components, it may be necessary to obtain additional information on chemical formulations, storage, drying times and airing procedures.

When specifying materials for interiors, special attention should be given to the stability of the materials, since this characteristic will impact the air quality for considerable time after the construction is completed. It is always good practice, especially for contract designs, to select interior finishes that do

MATERIAL SAFETY DATA SHEET - ENVIROTEC

Date of prep ___9/28/91___

NFPA HMIS H=0
F=0
R=0

HEALTHGUARD ADHESIVE #2093

SECTION I

Prepared by: Mel Nichols
Manufacturer's Name: W.F. Taylor Co. Inc.
Street Address: 13660 Excelsior Dr., Santa Fe Springs, CA 90670
Emergency Telephone No.: 1-800-535-5053
W.F. Taylor Telephone No.: (310) 802-1896
Product Class: Synthetic latex blend
Manufacturer's Code Identification: 2093P
Trade Name: Rubber Flooring Adhesive

SECTION II
HAZARDOUS INGREDIENTS

None per OSHA Regulation: 29 CFR 1910.1200
SARA Title III Section 313 Chemicals: None

SECTION III
PHYSICAL DATA

Boiling Point: 212 F
LBS/GAL: 10-12
Evaporation Rate: Same as water
Vapor Density: Same as water
Vapor Pressure: Same as water
Percent Volatile: 25-35 (by weight)
Color: Off White
Odor: Nil
Grams V.O.C. per liter of material: 0 (calculated)
Grams V.O.C. per liter of coating: 0 (calculated)

SECTION IV
FIRE AND EXPLOSION
HAZARD DATA

DOT Category: Not regulated
Flash Point: None
LEL: NA
Extinguishing Media: None required
Unusual Fire and Explosion Hazards: None Known
Special Fire Fighting Procedures: None Known

SECTION V
HEALTH HAZARD DATA

Symptoms of over exposure: None Known
Inhalation: None Known
Eyes: May cause mild irritation
Skin: None Known
Ingestion: None Known

SECTION VI
REACTIVITY DATA

Stability: Stable
Conditions to avoid: None Known
Incompatibility materials to avoid: None Known
Hazardous decomposition products: None Known
Hazardous polymerization: Will not occur
Conditions to avoid: None Known

SECTION VII
SPILL OR LEAK PROCEDURES

STEPS TO BE TAKEN IN CASE MATERIAL IS SPILLED
Use absorbent material to collect and contain for salvage or disposal
Waste disposal: Abide by all state, federal and local regulations

SECTION VIII
SPECIAL PROTECTION
INFORMATION

Respiratory protection: None should be needed
Ventilation: Local exhaust
Protective gloves: Not required
Eyes: Goggles
Other protective equipment: Not required

SECTION IX
SPECIAL PRECAUTIONS

Precaution for handling and storing:
Do not puncture   Keep out of reach of children
Freeze - thaw stable at 10°F

FIRST AID PROCEDURES

Eyes: Flush with water
Skin: Wash with soap and water
Inhalation: Remove to fresh air if needed

Fig. II-14:
Example of Manufacturers Safety Data Sheet. (Courtesy of W.F. Taylor Co. Inc.)

not produce or retain dust. Durable materials such as hardwoods, ceramics, masonry, metals, glass, baked enamels and hard plastics are generally low in VOC emissions. Many fibers such as cotton, wool, acetate and rayon also have low emissions, but their dyes and treatments can introduce toxic chemicals into the interior. It is also advisable to limit open shelving space to prevent dust accumulation.

For various reasons, including budget, it is often difficult to avoid the use of materials that potentially are not the best choices, for example, particleboard bonded with resin glues high in formaldehyde emissions. In these situations, precautions should be taken to limit the negative effects and at least reduce amounts of VOCs. In the case of particleboard, for example, the answer may be to seal the material with a secure coating that will encapsulate the VOCs.

Besides materials that may introduce harmful chemicals into the indoor environment, other types of indoor pollution are generated by various equipment. In most cases the equipment-specific pollution can be dealt with by proper enclosure and ventilation.

Electromagnetic emissions from VDTs present additional and unique concerns. When designing spaces where electronic equipment will be used there is an urgent need to redefine and redistribute the typical work space in order to avoid or, at least, minimize the harmful radiation. The radiation pattern of the computer is similar to that of a TV; however the computer operator sits much closer to the screen than a person watching television. The average field around computers is harmless at a distance of 30 to 40 in. (Fig. II-15). Sitting closer multiplies the hazard significantly. "At arm's length" has become the generally accepted, though unscientific, measurement for the spacing of computer screens. This is why the use of detachable keyboards is so

important. If sitting at "arm's length" from the front, sides or back of a monitor is to be a sensible solution, then designers have to double the space allocation per computer operating person. Finding the most economic spatial solution continues to be a challenge to the interior designer. One of the possibilities is arranging the stations, not in a straight line, but in a "zig-zag" manner (Fig. II-16).

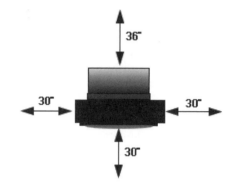

Fig.II-15:
The average extent of the electromagnetic field around a computer.

Fig. II-16:
One of the possibilities of arranging VDT stations.

(Source: Malino and Lee, pp. 74-75)

The magnetic field emissions are not stopped by cubicle partitions; on the contrary: "Recent studies actually show that partitions, especially those that carry circuitry in the base or cap, are potentially even more hazardous than the computer itself. These partitions set up an enormous field around the user and may actually amplify the fields" (Malino and Lee, p.75).

The safe electromagnetic field strength has not been established but, based on available research, several states have limited the maximum strength of electric and magnetic fields. There is still considerable uncertainty surrounding the issue of the effects of EMF on human health and more research needs to be done. Exposure to radiation can be reduced by buying expensive specially shielded monitors, or much more affordable anti-radiation screens. Some of today's manufactured stations have built-in controlling shields, or have reduced emissions display terminals.

Just as with equipment-specific pollution, pollution originating at the site of specific occupant activities should be localized and dealt with through enclosure and provision of local exhaust. That applies, for example, to cooking, personal hygiene, or smoking. As long as tobacco smoking is still present in the society, it is up to designers to remember to include in space planning for offices, institutions, gathering places, and so on, smoking lounges appropriately equipped with an efficient ventilation system. Disregarding this need leads to losses in productivity, or to smoking in less visible spaces, for example, fire escape stairways, which adds to unnecessary maintenance. If the entire building is a no smoking environment, the simple installation of few ashtrays outside the building seems to be a thoughtful provision.

VENTILATION

Controlling the sources of pollution is the most effective strategy for clean indoor air; ventilation, either natural or mechanical, is the second. Buildings are enclosed environments and regular air exchange is necessary to prevent the buildup of indoor pollution from both building related and occupant related

Side note:
"The recommended ventilation rate for most buildings is 20 cfm of outside air for each occupant in non-smoking areas .... Of the 20 cfm only 3 to 5 cfm are necessary for diluting carbon dioxide from human respiration and another 3 to 5 cfm for diluting body odors. The remaining 10 to 15 cfm is necessary for diluting emissions from interior building materials and office equipment" ("Global choices...," p.22).

sources. Appropriate ventilation not only removes polluted air, but also regulates the level of moisture in buildings.

Ventilation is usually defined as "introducing outside air to replace contaminated indoor air." Actually, ventilation is a combination of bringing in outdoor air, conditioning and mixing the outdoor air with some portion of indoor air, distributing this mixed air throughout the building, and exhausting some portion of the indoor air outside. A major step toward better indoor air quality has been taken with the publication of new ventilation standards in "Standard 62-1989: Ventilation for acceptable indoor air quality" by the American Society of Heating, Refrigeration and Air Conditioning Engineers (ASHRAE). The established voluntary standards require ventilation rates ranging from 15 to 60 cfm/person, depending on the activities that normally occur in that space. In addition, Standard 62-1989 includes provisions for dedicated local exhaust ventilation with industrial air change rates in specific areas such as printing, copying, smoking lounges, and so on.

In addition to the higher ventilation rate, the Standard includes many constructive strategies that building owners and managers, designers and occupants can use to improve indoor air quality. It is crucial, for example, that air handling systems are correctly installed, routinely inspected, that filters are changed when necessary and that ducts are cleaned and drained. For the city building or for buildings located near highways there is also a need for monitoring outdoor air quality. Bill Holdsworth and Anthony Sealey in *Healthy Buildings. A Design Primer for a Living Environment* proposed flexible ventilation systems that would take into consideration outside conditions and have:

- All ventilation intake openings sheltered and placed high up, if possible;
- Reduced air input during traffic rush hours;
- Reduced air input on days of heavy pollution or unfavorable wind direction in case of industrial pollution; and
- A plan for a protective belt of trees, bushes or climbing plants on walls.

When planning the layout of the furniture and furnishings, designers have to be careful not to obstruct air circulation. "Tall furniture, such as filing cabinets and acoustic screens, especially those that extend to the floor, even if they are no higher than 60 inches, may impede air circulation even if an adequate amount of air is being delivered to the space.... Because air handling for most office floors is designed for an open and unobstructed space,

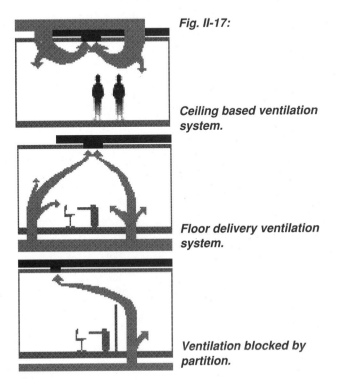

Fig. II-17:

Ceiling based ventilation system.

Floor delivery ventilation system.

Ventilation blocked by partition.

walls and partitions built to enclose work stations or meeting rooms can prevent the efficient flow of air" (Vischer, pp. 208-209). To ensure proper air circulation, the path of air delivered should not be interrupted, so it can move successfully through the interior. If privacy or acoustic partitions are used, they should clear the floor at their base to a height of 1 to 2 inches to allow air flow (some sources suggest a clearance of 6 inches). If walls or full-height partitions are used for enclosure, each enclosed space should have at least one supply vent and at least one return or exhaust vent.

To extract contaminants from localized sources it is necessary to provide local exhaust ventilation. Examples include an exhaust fan in a smoking lounge, a kitchen range fan or a bathroom fan. This kind of ventilation system when used for commercial interiors can exhaust contaminants from office equipment such as photocopiers, blueprinting machines, and so on. When properly designed and placed, the local exhaust system will remove pollution before it mixes with indoor air, allowing reduction of the overall building ventilation.

Additional air purification can be provided through the installation of air cleaners. Their sizes and types vary from small and simple tabletop models to sophisticated central systems. Air cleaners are mainly effective in removing particles–small solid or liquid substances suspended in the air, such as dust or light spray mist. To remove gaseous pollutants, air cleaners have to be equipped with special filtering materials, such as activated carbon or alumina, but even with such provisions, there is not enough data to assess the effect. The overall effectiveness of an air cleaner depends on its ability to collect pollutants from indoor air and on the amount of air (in cfm) drawn through the cleaning or filtering element. The effectiveness of an air cleaner can be totally compromised by an inadequate choice (too small a capacity for too large an area) or by lack of appropriate maintenance.

The humidity level in interior spaces is also controlled by proper ventilation. Too much or too little humidity can be a source of health complaints: excessive moisture can support growth of bacteria, viruses and fungi, excessive dryness increases airborne dust and causes respiratory reactions including allergic and asthmatic symptoms. Outside vented exhaust fans are very effective in controlling humidity when properly placed in those areas which produce the most wetness such as kitchens and bathrooms. For excessive dryness, especially during winter, it may be necessary to install electronic humidifiers, or furnace register humidifiers.

A new generation of office systems is based on work stations at which each person can control individually the amount of heat and air exchanges. The benefits of increased productivity quickly pay for the initial investment, as seen in the example of the new offices of West Bend Mutual Insurance Company (see: "Case Study", pp. 134-137).

Even the most sophisticated, well designed ventilation systems can become a source of contamination, or cease to provide fresh air if they are not properly maintained. Every ventilation system or air cleaner needs periodic inspection, cleaning and filter replacement. If appropriate air quality control measures are used, such as reducing sources of indoor air pollution, ensuring local exhaust of pollution sources, periodic monitoring and providing appropriate maintenance, buildings can become truly clean air buildings.

Side note:
There are companies specializing in products that help curb "sick building syndrome" through air filtration systems for offices, systems that remove airborne particulates, including dust, tobacco smoke, bacteria, pollen, spores, viruses and other contaminants. These filtration systems suck in ambient air and release the filtered air over the work stations ("Environmentally Concerned...," p. 19).

Side note:
"Making informed choices concerning the types of products and materials purchased and their use, properly caring for and maintaining potential sources such as combustion devices, and appropriately balancing indoor air quality and energy concerns in ventilation practices are examples of decisions and actions that can significantly improve indoor air quality" (US EPA, "Report to ...," p.4).

PLANTS

The benefits of trees, bushes, and other plants surrounding buildings are unquestionable. They provide shading, which allows for better control of sunlight and indoor climate, they build up natural protection from air and noise pollution, and, last but not least, plants are, by most people, recognized as a visually pleasurable experience. Recent research proved that plants can also be used indoors as air filters, and that one of the ways to fight indoor air pollution can be as simple as bringing plants into the interior.

Studies by the National Aeronautics & Space Administration (NASA) done in the late 1980s drew a link between plants and air pollutants. The published studies describe how certain species of common office plants reduced levels of toxic gases in air chambers under controlled conditions.

Fig. II-18:
Ford Foundation Building: garden in the internal courtyard.
(Photo: H. Stern.)

According to the NASA researchers, plants absorb airborne pollutants as part of photosynthesis, a process in which plants take in carbon dioxide and release oxygen and water vapor through tiny openings on leaves. Among those plants tested, some "specialize" in the removal of particular pollutants. For example dendrobium orchids and bromeliads are very effective in "cleaning" the air of acetone, methyl alcohol, ethyl acetate and xylene. Philodendrons have the greatest overall filtering abilities and formaldehyde is effectively removed by banana trees, green spider plant, or golden pothos. Adding activated carbon to the potting soil and providing fan-powered air movement across the plant appear to be particularly effective in trapping contaminants. The microbial organisms in the soil digest the contaminants and regenerate the activated carbon. Plants are the most effective as air filters when used

POLLUTANT	SOURCES	SOLUTIONS
formaldehyde	foam insulation	Chrysanthemum
	plywood	Azalea
	particle board	Dieffenbachia
	carpeting	Philodendron
	furniture	Spider plant
	clothes	Golden pothos
	paper goods	Bamboo palm
	household cleaners	Corn plant
	water repellents	Mother-in-law's tongue
benzene	synthetic fibers	Chrysanthemum
	plastics	Gerbera daisy
	inks	Marginata
	tobacco smoke	Peace lily
	oils	Warneckei
	rubber	Janet Craig
	detergents	English ivy
trichloroethylene	paints	Chrysanthemum
	varnishes	Gerbera daisy
	lacquers	Marginata
	adhesives	Peace lily
	inks	Warneckei

Fig. II-19:
Plants "specializing" in absorption of various pollutants (Source: "Notes on the…," p.85).

in a space with adequate ventilation and well-maintained HVAC systems.

Bringing plants into interiors and providing for their healthy growth will, however, increase maintenance tasks. Plants, like humans, require the correct balance of light, water, temperature and nourishment. Plants require a different amount and

Fig. II-20:
"The Foliage for Clean Air Council suggest that one potted plant per 100 sq.ft. of floor area can effectively remove pollutants from the air" ("Notes on the...," p. 85).

quality of light than do people: most plants need as much as four times the amount of light acceptable for people, and the light has to have a full spectrum. Tinted glass, for example, while not limiting the amount of light, may change its spectral quality and affect the plant's ability to grow. Spaces with significant amounts of plants have to be monitored for moisture, since the presence of plants may increase water content in the air. Bringing plants into the interior has to be a thoughtful process and requires initial research to establish the most beneficial species that will function well in the particular space.

Further field tests of the plant-as-air-filter proved that the plants cannot be treated as a quick solution to sick building syndrome. More elements have to be addressed to clean the indoor air. But it is appropriate to say that in addition to aesthetic and stress-reducing psychological values, plants also help to clean the air.

FINISHING AND MAINTENANCE

Interior finishing and maintenance operations pose the greatest hazard of exposure to volatile organic compounds. Designers can and should encourage appropriate methods to alleviate the VOCs' impact on construction workers and building occupants. If renovation is taking place in an occupied building, it is very important to securely isolate the work area from the occupied interiors. It is also important to supply temporary extra ventilation using window or door mounted fans. There are also organic vapor respirators available, certified by OHSA/NIOSH/WCB, with charcoal filters that effectively remove vapors.

The period immediately following interior finishing operations is critical for VOC exposure. If possible, the best practice is to delay occupancy to allow "outgassing"–the release of harmful components from adhesives, paints and other building and interior materials and finishes. In some cases, mainly with new construction, it is possible to use a "bakeout period." During this process an unoccupied building is sealed and the temperature is raised to about 80° F; periodically the building is thoroughly ventilated. The bakeout period, which should last from 72 hours to a week, can substantially increase the aging rate for many of the shorter lived sources of VOCs, but it has to be done thoughtfully and be professionally monitored.

Many decisions about maintenance requirements are made while planning, designing and constructing the space. It is the designer's responsibility to educate building owners, managers and maintenance staff about this single most important factor in assuring the consistent functioning of the interior. Some of the important information that will help provide appropriate maintenance of interiors is as follows:

Side note:
"A building is like a person in that its components grow old and decay. In the same way that we stay healthy by keeping fit and clean, so also a building must be kept clean... [and] subject to periodic checks for repair and maintenance. ... Without proper care a healthy building will soon become sick" (Holdsworth and Sealey, p.9).

- The people who will be responsible for maintenance and management must understand the original design elements and principles if future benefits are to result from a responsible design.

- Maintenance and monitoring of the HVAC system reduces the chances of a "healthy" building becoming "sick" and assures that problems can be identified and corrected at minimal expense. There are devices available that function as controllers of HVAC equipment. Based on sensing the concentration of different pollutants, these devices can help in identifying existing or potential problems.

- Yearly maintenance of electrical equipment, in particular, lighting, can result in 25 percent more light while using the same amount of energy. Part of any energy efficiency program is keeping fixtures and lamps clean.

- In general, to control microbial contamination the only major protection is the incorporation of a broad spectrum antimicrobial additive. After that, the next step is a maintenance issue: keeping the interior clean, free of humidity and well ventilated.

- The effect of carefully chosen finishes and materials may be totally lost if maintenance requirements are not considered. Low VOC emission products may become sources of indoor pollution if their cleaning requires highly toxic solvents.

- It is a learning experience for interior designers to come back to the space they designed a few months after the construction was finished, and maybe a few years later as well. Going through the evaluation process and getting feedback from environmental consultant on the performance of the interior will help to improve future projects. There are a variety of air quality and toxicity tests that can be used to evaluate indoor air.

It is important to understand that maintenance is part of the conservation of a building and not an odd-job performed when replacement of defective parts is necessary. Many buildings become sick due to a lack of proper maintenance. A combination of dust, microorganisms, dirty ducts, clogged-up filters in ventilation systems, chemicals used for "quick-fix" cleaning of carpet or upholstery, and so on, all may add up and become a "cocktail" of indoor air pollution dangerous to human health.

Additional information

More in-depth analysis can be found in:

• Concerning standards for contaminants:
United States Environmental Protection Agency (EPA). 1991. "Introduction to Indoor Air Quality. A Reference Manual." EPA/400/3-91/003. Washington, DC.

• Concerning EMF:
United States Environmental Protection Agency (EPA). 1990. "Evaluation of the Potential Carcinogenicity of Electromagnetic Fields, Draft Report." Washington DC.

• Concerning ventilation:
United States Environmental Protection Agency (EPA). 1991. "Introduction to Indoor Air Quality. A Reference Manual." EPA/400/3-91/003. Washington, DC.

• Concerning analysis of air cleaners:
United States Environmental Protection Agency (EPA). 1990. "Residential Air Cleaners." EPA/20A-4001/2-90. Washington, DC.

CHAPTER 5
MATERIALS AND PRODUCTS

*"What architects [and interior
designers] might expect - a simple manual or
checklist to consult - is precisely what green
leaders say they shouldn't have. 'People
can't just take a list of stuff and say "these
are green materials; use them,"' says Kirsten
Childs, explaining that products change and
that no list can be authoritative."*
(Branch, p. 76).

The 1990s brought considerable changes in the
general attitude toward environmental issues. Public
concern for the environment escalated during the
1980s, and the economic power of the "green consumer" has proven particularly effective in promoting that change.

When shopping for "green products," that is
products that do not pollute indoor air and whose
production processes, and later functioning, cause as
little damage to the global environment as possible,
designers may find it difficult, if at all possible, to
verify the producers' claims of any product being
environmentally friendly. The producer's record on
environmental issues affects businesses, especially
larger companies, since their actions and presence
are more visible, and negative associations may
lower sales of products and affect prices of company
stock. With increasing awareness of the environmental damage caused by the industry, consumers'
preferences are often altered. Sometimes, companies
choose to advertise the environmental benefits, but
omit information about the overall environmental
impact of the product. That's why more and more, not
only environmental groups, but also conscientious

professionals realize the necessity to educate the design community and to develop, sponsor and use independent sources of information about products.

The following descriptions of materials and groups of products used in interior projects are intended only as a guide to selecting environmentally friendly materials and products. They point out the main characteristics as they relate to the impact on the environment. With this core of information, the designer can begin to develop questions that should be directed to particular manufacturers and suppliers. **No endorsement or advertisement of any manufacturers or products is intended.**

Side note:
"[Choosing materials and products] is not as easy as buying bumper stickers with catchy slogans. Conscientious buying takes hard work and a certain amount of investigation" (Stark, p.1).

LIFE CYCLE ANALYSIS

Products and materials used in interiors are called "green" when they do not contribute to indoor air pollution, which means they do not compromise the health of the occupants, and, at the same time, their production processes, useful life and disposal cause as little damage to the global environment as possible. A very helpful tool to evaluate the impact of a material or a product on the global environment is its life cycle analysis. If the analysis is complete and examines the entire life of a material or product up to a point of disposal it is called "cradle to grave." If a material's or product's life does not end with disposal, but through the recycling processes becomes the source of a new product, then the analysis is often called "cradle to cradle." These life cycle analyses include a close look at every step: extraction or acquisition of the raw material, production processes, transportation/distribution, packaging, use, and disposal or reuse/recycling.

Listed below are examples of the questions that should be asked when deciding about specifying materials or products:

• Is the source of the raw material renewable, non-renewable, depleted or sustainably managed?
• Does the acquisition of the raw material impact negatively on the environment?
• Are the production processes polluting water, air or soil, or affecting the environment in any other negative way (i.e., upsetting ecological balance)?
• How much waste is produced during the manufacturing processes?
• How toxic are the by-products and waste from the manufacturing processes?
• How far does the material/product have to travel before it reaches its final destination?
• What are the packaging requirements and what toll on the environment do they cause?
• How much refinishing, dry cleaning, shampooing and other maintenance materials will be used over the material or product's life and how do they influence the IAQ (what is the environ-

Fig. II-21:
Life cycle chart.

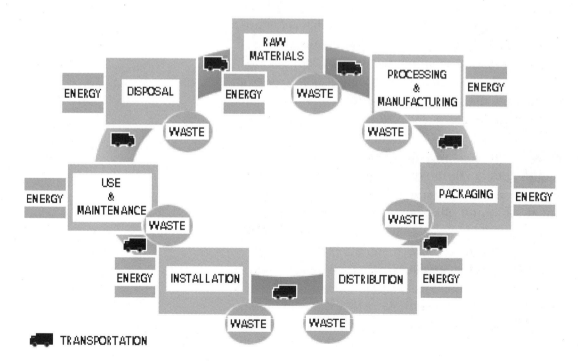

mental cost of those maintenance materials?)
• What is the replacement cycle?
• What portion of the material is likely to become waste; is it toxic, and what can be done with it?
• Is the production, installation or use of the material or product in any way compromising the health of people involved?
• How much energy is required at every step of the material's or product's life listed above?

One of the most important concepts in life cycle analysis is the energy content or embodied energy. The energy content represents all of the energy involved in all of the processes throughout the material's or product's life cycle, starting with the acquisition of the raw materials, the manufacturing, packaging, and distribution of the product. Embodied energy or energy content, quantified in BTUs per weight unit, is a useful measure of the environmental impact of a material. For example, the use of locally produced materials can significantly reduce the burden on the environment by eliminating extensive transportation. Also, an

Fig. II-22:
Embodied energy in various materials in relation to wood's 639 kilowatt-hours per ton.
(Source: Ramsey and Sleeper, 1993, p.283.)

analysis of the energy content will quickly show the benefits of renovating buildings as opposed to their demolition and replacement with new construction.

SYNTHETICS VERSUS NATURAL MATERIALS

In general, the choice of natural materials over synthetics is influenced by the knowledge that some of them, such as plant fibers, are derived from renewable sources. Natural materials usually require less of a "manufacturing" process, so their production involves less air and water pollution, as well as less "embodied energy." Most natural materials also bring fewer toxicity problems than man-made products.

Often, however, opinions about synthetic materials are based on prejudice rather than facts. Attention is usually focused on the main sources of materials or products, without taking into account the entire processing chain or the final performance. For example, an analysis of the choice between wood and a recycled plastic product for outside installation may not favor the natural material, since the particular species of wood may be extinct, or require toxic chemical treatment for outdoor use. Specifying wool carpet opens plenty of questions about finishing, and cleaning chemicals that will affect indoor air quality. Not all natural materials are better for the environment than man-made.

To properly judge which product is more appropriate designers have to consider the whole life cycle. All materials exact some environmental toll in their production. Natural fibers may come from pesticide-intensive crops, which are more damaging to the environment than many manufacturing processes. Growing and processing cotton, for example, may involve high costs of soil depletion, fertilizer and pesticide use and pollution of water and air. Thoughtless wood harvesting brings environmental problems in the tropical forests of the Amazon, in coastal forests of Oregon and Washington, and results in global changes in weather patterns, air quality, and water distribution. There is no simple answer. Each decision involves educated questions directed to the suppliers or producers, and, unfortunately, sometimes just choosing the lesser evil.

WOOD PRODUCTS

Timber

The basic division between woods used in the industry defines them as hardwoods and softwoods.

Most hardwoods are slow growing and cannot sustain rapid increase in demand. The most popular domestic hardwoods include: alder, apple, ash, aspen, beech, birch, cherry, elm, gum, hickory, lime, maple, oak red or white, pear, poplar, sycamore, walnut and whitewood. They are used in furniture and cabinetry manufacturing; some are also used as flooring materials. The most depleted of the naturally grown domestic hardwoods are cherry and walnut.

Softwoods grow much faster than hardwoods. The most popular softwoods include: cedar, fir, hemlock, larch, pine, redwood and spruce. They are cut domestically or in Europe and are used sometimes for furniture manufacturing, but more often for construction. Cedar and rosewood are the slowest to regenerate and are rapidly diminishing. Softwoods are sometimes a problem for people with allergies because they contain volatile resins (terpines).

The list of endangered woods and their origins is long, but designers should be using that list on an everyday basis and should avoid specifying species

whose extinction threatens the global ecology. Woodworkers Alliance for Rainforest Protection, Coos Bay, Oregon, provides information on environmentally responsible sources of wood for wood users, and cautions that lists easily become outdated. They urge consumers to ask questions.

The list below is not complete; it is just a sampler.

WOODS TO AVOID:

(Source: "Notes…," pp.83-84, and "Commmonly…," p.2)

TROPICAL

AFRICAN TEAK–also called iroko or kambala–from Liberia, Ghana, Ivory Coast.
EBONY–also called batulinau–from West Africa, India, East Indies, Malaysia, Indonesia and the Philippines.
FIJI BIRCH–dakua makadre or dakua salusalu from Fiji.
MAHOGANY–African from West Africa;
  –white mahogany–called avoidire, imported from Ivory Coast;
  –American–Honduras mahogany, tropical American mahogany from Mexico, Central and South America;
  –Philippine mahogany called also meranti, seraya or lauan from Southeast Asia.
OAK–tropical–roble and encino from Mexico and South America.
PURPLEHEART–amaranth–from Brazil, Mexico, Central America.
ROSEWOOD–Indian from Brazil, Honduras, India and Ceylon;
  –Amazon, Brazilian known as jacaranda, palisander, marnut;
  –from Honduras called also nagaed wood;
  –from Mexico, Central America and Colombia–called Cocobolo or Nicaraguan rosewood.
SPANISH CEDAR–from Central America and northern South America–called cedro.
TEAK–from Burma, Thailand, Indonesia and Cambodia.
ZEBRAWOOD–from Nigeria, West Africa.

TEMPERATE

DOUGLAS FIR–Oregon pine, yellow fir, red fir from Western US, Mexico, Canada. Yellow fir comes from old-growth forests which are 95% depleted in North America.

REDWOOD–sequoia from Northern California, southern Oregon.
WESTERN RED CEDAR–called also canoe cedar, giant arborvitae, shingle wood, Pacific red cedar–from Washington, Oregon, Idaho and Montana.

"Rather than considering the forest as a mine to be plundered in order to make products, we have to start designing our products around what the forest is willing to give us" says William McDonough, architect, activist, and great advocate of sustainable forestry (Wagner, "Natural resources," p.60). Most interior designers tend to want to see the same options of wood offered year after year. If furniture companies are to gear their production to what the forest can provide on a sustainable basis, that attitude has to change. Designers need to learn to use lesser known species to replace depleted resources.

Fig. II-23:
American redwoods in Northern California.
(Photo: author.)

Architectural wood products

Architectural wood products, including particleboard or simulated wood paneling, make good use of low quality raw materials and can be made from recycled wood, but these standard materials are usually bonded with resin glues, which are one of the major sources of formaldehyde indoors. A few manufacturers now offer "low emission" or "formaldehyde free" alternatives. In general, exterior grade plywood and sheathing boards are made with a lower emission glue. "Aging" of particleboard in a heated shop for a few months can also limit emissions, and then all faces and edges can be thoroughly sealed with a laminate material or a varnish type sealer.

Another concern involved with construction grade softwoods is the anti-sapstain treatment applied to green lumber before shipping. The softwoods are treated with a toxic copper compound mixed with other agents to reduce fungus growth on green lumber. The chemicals present a serious hazard, especially to mill-workers and carpenters. These treatments are now being replaced by safer borax-based compounds. It is good advice to specify kiln dried lumber for construction, although this process uses a significant amount of energy.

Furniture

Among the imported hardwoods, teak, rosewood and mahogany are the most commonly used in furniture manufacturing. They are, however, expensive and depleted. There are varieties of less known hardwoods that could be used in their place, including locally ranch grown poplar, birch or cherry. If necessary, the appearance of wood can be altered or adjusted for specific effects by staining.

Particleboard, the major source of formaldehyde indoors, is very difficult to avoid, especially when working within a limited budget. In this situation, designers should select particleboard that causes the least air pollution. This information can be obtained from the manufacturers, if they have done emissions testing. The more designers and architects demand testing, the more industry will be pressed to conduct it. If the emission testing is not available, designers can look for manufacturers who are using "European standard" board, which has lower emissions, or board which is rated "exposure one" under US emissions rules. When using furniture with particleboard sealed with veneers or laminate materials, it is important to check to see that all surfaces are completely sealed, especially edges, backs, under desk or table tops, inside cabinets and drawers. If deficiencies exist, it is possible to request an application of a liquid sealer formulated especially for formaldehyde reduction.

With increasing awareness of limited supplies of wood in the world, in addition to searching for environmentally sound timber, some furniture designers and manufacturers are coming up with ideas for using recycled wood to build furniture, for example, using wood from pallets or discarded redwood wine vats. The use of reconditioned furniture is another way to limit the strain on the environment, as well as lower the cost and prevent unnecessary waste. There are more and more firms specializing in renovating and selling secondhand, or surplus residential and commercial furniture.

Veneers and wood finishes

One way of preserving precious, endangered species of wood is to use veneers. Many manufacturers are using a low cost, stable core-wood

Side note:
Good choices of materials are bamboo, wicker or Indonesian rattan. Bamboo is fast growing and in plentiful supply. True wicker is made from twigs of willows, which grow in northern temperate climates and are not depleted. Rattan is made from several hundred species of palms growing in tropical forests. Since 1988, Indonesia has imposed a ban on exporting all raw materials to encourage manufacture of furniture in their country, which has been largely successful in developing industry. Although it is a depleted resource in many areas, buying rattan goods from Indonesia helps to encourage manufacturing by the producer nation.

(such as alder or birch) and applying high quality hardwood veneers to them. The best veneers are "ribbon cut" in matched sheets.

Another way of satisfying aesthetic requirements is dyeing or staining less attractive woods, which if done in a creative way, may bring desirable results and add interest to the wood's appearance.

Fig. II-24:
The Knoll Group, the office-furnishings manufacturer, works with Scientific Certification Systems, previously Green Cross, to identify and use only wood grown in a way that doesn't degrade and destroy the rain forest. The whole new series of woven bentwood furniture designed by architect Frank Gehry is produced from sustainable sources approved as such by Scientific Certification System.
Herman Miller stopped using tropical rosewood veneer for its Eames chairs when its current stock dried up and switched to domestic walnut or cherry veneers over molded plywood.

(Photomontage by H. Pancewicz; photos courtesy of: The Knoll Group–Power Play chair and ottoman; Herman Miller Inc.–Eames Lounge; Aris Multimedia Entertainment, Inc.,1993–background rain forest.)

The most polluting processes in the wood industry are painting and plating. Both produce extensive air and water pollution and toxic waste, and are serious health hazards for workers. Some furniture manufacturers have switched to coating processes, which cause less pollution and are safer. Those processes include metal coating, called also "powder coating," and polymer coating, which replaced air and water polluting cadmium plating.

PLASTICS

The most important raw material needed for the production of plastic is nonrenewable petroleum. Besides the very complex political and economic situation created by the demand for this resource, reckless transportation and off-shore drilling of petroleum are the sources of the worst man-made environmental disasters.

Most of the public perceive plastics as true solids, but chemists describe plastics as viscoelastic fluids and explain that, like every other fluid, plastics evaporate. This is why, in many ways, plastics degrade as soon as they are produced. Wallcoverings, carpets, padding, plumbing, electrical wire and insulation made with plastics, emit toxic chemicals– nitrogen oxide, cyanide, acid gases, and so on. The toxic fumes can actually be produced not by plastic itself, but by polymers or additives used as colorants or plasticizers. The degradation, which causes evaporation, is susceptible to environmental stresses: air, light, pressure and heat. To control plastics emissions, it is not necessary to stop using them, but rather to understand the nature of various plastics and to specify them appropriately to their function.

There are two main categories of plastics: soft and rigid. Soft plastics, which contain plasticizers, tend to be less stable. Some plastics are safe for use

in interiors, for example, PVCs (polyvinyl chlorides), but the process of their production creates industrial hazards and health risks during manufacturing. They are also highly toxic in case of fire. Most plastic laminates used for cabinet surfaces have a very low toxicity, but, since they are made out of petroleum, their manufacturing often causes various forms of pollution.

Until recently, plastic upholstery foams and rigid insulating foams have been produced using ozone depleting CFCs or toxic methylene chloride. New technologies have replaced CFCs, but the substitutes present other environmental hazards. For example, HCFCs–hydrofluorocarbons, ozone-safer CFC substitutes–are one of the most active "heat trapping" agents, contributing significantly to the greenhouse effect.

The biggest problem created by plastics is their indestructible quality; plastics will last for hundreds of years after they have been discarded. Plastics are the most common man-made objects polluting the marine environment. To turn disadvantage into advantage, the best solution is recycling, which puts back into use previously made plastics, saving a great deal of both raw materials and embodied energy. Recycling plastics limits solid waste and saves other resources; unfortunately, it is still very limited. There have been some initiatives and it is now possible to buy some outdoor furniture, floor tiles and carpets made out of recycled plastics. Hopefully these initiatives will prove successful and invite other industries.

TEXTILES

As with wood, there is no easy answer to the question: What is the most environmentally friendly fiber or the "greenest" textile? Once again, the whole

process has to be considered, from fiber production through fabric finishing.

"Natural fibers biodegrade and are produced by agricultural processes which–despite the use of pesticides and fertilizers–appear to be more environmentally friendly than the image of factories producing synthetics. However, such judgments cannot be made by comparing products alone. Understandably, consumers do not have sufficient knowledge about the textile processes involved; therefore their judgments are based upon narrow and incomplete information. So, in the pursuit of a neat answer to the question 'which is the most environmentally friendly fiber?' they have concluded that it must be natural fibers. The industry knows that these conclusions are incorrect" (Watson, p.7).

Natural resources are used in the production of all fibers–both natural and man-made. The manufacture of textiles involves extensive use of water and energy in all the processing stages. Production of man-made fibers consumes more energy than the production of raw natural fiber, but natural fibers need cleaning, transporting, and extensive dyeing and finishing, both of which are notorious for water pollution.

A comparison between the production processes of a petroleum-based synthetic fiber and cotton, illustrates the difficulties in judgment. Manufacturing synthetic fibers depletes nonrenewable resources, but the amount of petroleum used is negligible and the production processes are essentially clean. Cotton, which is made from a renewable resource (plants), requires a significant amount of pesticides and its production process causes extensive water pollution.

The production of man-made fiber is fairly clean with the exception of viscose. While the end product, viscose, is biodegradable and the raw material required for production is a renewable resource, the

process generates highly polluting air and water emissions.

The textile industry's most devastating impact on the environment is the finishing process. Finishing includes dyeing, sizing and treating for stain and wrinkle resistance, mildew, fire and mothproofing, and so on. Cotton, of all fabrics, tends to be the most treated, and the sizing found on cotton is usually made with very irritating formaldehyde and latex polymers. The dyes and stain resistance treatments also contain many chemicals that are hazardous to produce and handle. They can cause skin reactions in people with sensitive skin.

There are natural dyes available, but it is not possible to turn back to totally natural dyes since demand would outstrip supply and the superior performance of synthetic dyes would make the use of natural dyes unacceptable. Natural dyes are also not totally pollution-free and they require use of a mordant–very toxic metallic compounds–which increases dye fastness. In addition, the use of natural dyes is restricted to natural fibers.

Many fibers are developed for specific uses and there are few opportunities for fiber substitution within market sectors. The highly specialized characteristics of one fiber cannot be matched by others. This is especially true for man-made fibers, which can produce yarns generally much lighter than natural fibers, while maintaining their strength. Sometimes, the properties of natural fibers are enhanced by the addition of man-made fibers in yarns: nylon is mixed with wool to provide greater strength and durability.

One way of raising awareness and encouraging sales of "green textiles" would be the introduction of a special labeling system. Labels would make it clear which products have been produced by factories that cause as little damage to the environment as possible.

Acetates and rayons are synthetic fibers but made from digested wood and plant fiber. Nylon, polyesters, acrylics and polypropylene are usually made from petroleum, though most could be made from wood and plant fiber with different manufacturing methods.

LEATHER

Most of the leather used in interior design is produced from animals slaughtered for meat, and prevents the waste of that part of the animal. Hopefully, animal growers provided for cruelty-free environments while raising cattle or pigs. As with dyeing textiles, the tanning and dyeing of leather have serious environmental consequences, due to the use of alkalis, chromium compounds and other toxic materials. In most countries, tannery discharges are now fairly well regulated, but, for example, in India or Brazil, unregulated tanneries provide a cheap service to overseas companies at the expense of local workers' health and safety. Skins of wild animals are banned by import/export restrictions all together, but unfortunately they are still occasionally the object of illegal trade.

An additional environmental problem to consider when using leather is maintenance: leather, especially suede and chamois, require highly polluting, chemical cleaning processes.

FLOOR COVERINGS

Carpets and rugs

Carpets are made of synthetic or natural fibers. The most often used synthetic fibers include nylon, polypropylene and a few polyesters; the main natural fibers are linens and wool. The backings are usually

Side note:
Cotton, wool, silk and linen are the major textiles made directly from renewable natural fibers. Recently, organically grown (without use of chemical fertilizers and pesticides) cottons have shown up on the market. It is also possible to buy cottons dyed with vegetable dyes and cottons bred and grown with natural colors. What seems like an amazing phenomena is actually a rediscovery of cottons which were grown by the native peoples of Central America hundreds of years ago. They are available in several earth tone colors.

polypropylene mesh or jute with a latex rubber bonding agent, with sometimes a secondary backing made of hemp.

Traditional carpets and handmade rugs are entirely loomed or knotted together and do not rely on the latex bonding agent. Some new carpet processes use a heat fusion bond for the backing, which eliminates the high VOC latex bond. Most carpets are also treated with stain and fire resistance agents. Wool carpet does not need, nor does it generally have, stain surface treatment, but must be mothproofed to carry the Woolmark® label. Wool and sisal carpets also have the advantage of being made of renewable materials.

Carpets, particularly the latex bonded varieties, are known to produce a wide range of volatile compounds, which have been the cause of complaints in cases of building related illness, both in homes and offices. One volatile agent, 4-PC, was recently isolated and may be the major cause of lingering "new carpet odor." Standards for 4-PC exposure or other carpet emissions have not yet been established and little information exists on how long the emissions last. Independent research on the health effects of carpet emissions is not available. Research done by fiber manufacturers found no adverse effects in rats exposed to inhalation of the maximum levels of 4-PC possible in air.

At this time, the best advice is to insure adequate ventilation and carpet maintenance. Generally, it is good practice to look for "low emission" carpets, fusion bonded backing, and alternative fastening systems to eliminate latex and adhesives. After installation, it is very important to allow the appropriate time (three to four weeks) for off-gassing. During that time, additional ventilation, that is, increased air exchange rate, will add to the off-gassing period's effectiveness.

Maintenance is another problem associated with the use of carpets; no matter how scrupulous the cleaning, carpets are always, for good and bad, a cesspool for particles and dust. In addition, most cleaning solutions for carpets, as for many other finishes, may introduce highly toxic chemicals to the interior. Vacuuming is the best way of controlling particles and dust, but, to be truly effective, it should be done with special dust-bags that retain microscopic particles. When interior designers specify carpets they have to take into consideration the function of the space and maintenance requirements, and choose the appropriate floor treatment accordingly.

The EPA and the Consumer Product Safety Commission have looked at carpets in recent years, especially since 1986, when an "infamous" carpet installation in EPA headquarters in Washington was believed to have caused health problems among agency employees. Both agencies, with the active cooperation and support of the carpet industry, acting through the Carpet and Rug Institute, continue their routine collection of information. The CRI has developed an Indoor Air Quality Testing Program to ensure that carpet is environmentally responsible. Such carpets, after a series of various tests and evaluations, are identified with a CRI IAQ label.

Fig. II-25:
The Carpet and Rug Institute Indoor Air Quality label.
(Courtesy of The Carpet and Rug Institute.)

Side note:
Special attention should be given to the choice of carpet for installation in areas where moisture may be prevalent such as laundries and around swimming pools. A good choice is, for example, carpet made of olefin, since this fiber is moisture and mildew resistant.

Side note:
Du Pont, a synthetic fiber manufacturer, together with carpet mills and carpet dealers, built up the Partnership for Carpet Reclamation. The Partnership focuses on the collection of post-consumer carpets and the development of the technology allowing for recycling.
Another synthetic fiber manufacturer, BASF, also implemented a nationwide commercial carpets recycling program in 1994.

Side note:
Jute backing was used in the Croxton Collaborative showcase projects: Environmental Defense Fund Offices, Natural Resources Defense Council and National Audubon Society (see Case Studies, pp. 130-133).

Approximately 3 billion yards of carpet are sold every year in the USA, about 70 percent of which is replacement carpet. This means that over 2 billion yards of carpet are sent each year to landfills, where they will remain, largely intact, for hundreds of years. The chemical industry is now working on nylon formulations that can be recycled into useful products again. Also, some manufacturers are now making a synthetic carpet fiber from recycled post-consumer plastics such as soft drink bottles.

Carpet pads and glues

Typical carpet pads are made of foamed plastic or sheet rubber. Both materials cause high emissions of VOCs. The low emission alternatives for carpet padding are felt pads, made from recycled synthetic fiber or wool, and, the best choice, jute backing, which can be tacked rather then glued down. Cork, another renewable, quickly growing natural resource, can also be used as carpet padding. Standard particleboard, a source of formaldehyde emissions, is often used as carpet underlayment, but should be avoided and replaced with exterior grade plywood or formaldehyde free particleboard. The best choice for underlayment is low density panels made from recycled paper.

For good indoor air quality, it is always a better choice to use nail strips and avoid any gluing. If glue must be used, water or low-toxic based varieties are safer for both the installer and the future occupants of the space.

Ceramics, stone, brick and other materials

Ceramics, stone, brick, terrazzo, slate and marble are all excellent high-end floor coverings. They are durable and chemically safe, especially when sealed with silicone or water-based acrylic sealers. "Glass bonded" floor tiles, which contain 70 percent recycled glass, make use of already processed materials. Always beneficial for the environment is the use of ceramic or stone tiles made from local materials and locally manufactured.

Vinyl and linoleum

Hard vinyl tile and traditional linoleum are durable, low cost, and low maintenance floor coverings. Soft vinyl, which is made out of petrochemical polymers, with chemicals added for flexibility, produces extensive volatile compounds for long periods of time. In contrast, natural linoleum is made of linseed oil, cork, tree resin, wood flour, clay pigments and a jute backing. It is a very durable flooring material which comes in a variety of colors.

PAINTS AND ADHESIVES
(Paints, varnishes, oil finishes, stains, adhesives and caulkings)

When deciding which paint to use, it is important to remember that paint consists of three elements and each of the three may compromise the environment.

Pigments, derived from various minerals or synthetic organic substances, are suspended in a vehicle or binder. The vehicle is usually a synthetic resin (polymer) dissolved in a solvent. The two main categories of available paints are solvent-based, usually called oil or lacquer, and water emulsions, called latex or acrylic latex. Solvent-based paints are more durable but they include hydrocarbons and other VOCs. Solvents evaporate as the paint dries, react with sunlight and pollutants in the air, and produce ozone. Solvent-based paints also require hazardous solvents for clean up and thinning. In Europe, solvent-free paints have been used for several years.

Side note:
"A recent investigation of five Danish Schools was made between the use of carpets, and their removal. ... The results showed that with fiber carpets the amount of settled dust ranged from 1,200 mg/square meter to 230 mg/square meter for a reasonably newly laid carpet. Good-quality linoleum gave a low reading of 65 mg/square meter" (Holdsworth and Sealey, p. 60).

Water-based paints are less hazardous to handle, but they contain biocidal agents to prevent fungus growth and spoilage. In indoor applications, the main difference in performance between water- and solvent-based paints is in scrub-resistance.

The Clean Air Act of 1990 puts the responsibility on the Federal Government to issue rules that would limit VOCs in paints. Without legislation, some of the manufacturers started voluntarily to limit VOC levels. "Environmentally friendly" paints re-formulate conventional latex paints and use low toxic pigments, omitting some of the biocides and stabilizers. Some of these paints are made entirely from plant materials and stable minerals and satisfy even very rigorous European standards. Information about VOC levels can be found on the paint's labels. A good reading is below 100 grams per liter.

Most varnishes are solvent-based urethanes. They are highly noxious to handle, but stable once cured. Recently, it has become possible to find water-based emulsion urethanes that are low-emission and that have performance as good as solvent-based.

Polymer oils for floor and cabinet finishing pro-duce hazardous formaldehyde gas, which remains toxic for several weeks after application. If the use of finishing oil is unavoidable, the better choices are water-based urethane, low toxic sealers and wax finishes.

Stains have similar qualities to water- and sol-vent-based paints. There are stains available that contain no toxic ingredients and are colored with natural minerals.

Adhesives are either solvent- or water-based. Solvent-based adhesives contain xylene, toluene, acetone or other hazardous solvents; water-based adhesives are safer to handle, though they also con-tain some solvents. The lowest in toxicity is water soluble casein or PVA-based plain white glue. This glue is easy to handle and suitable for woods, paper, leather, and so on.

Caulkings used indoors are generally latex or silicone types. Silicone is a very safe and stable low toxic material; latex caulks are also safe, but a few of them produce odors for weeks after installation. The most harmful are uncured rubber caulkings such as butyle, acoustical sealant and polysufide.

MISCELLANEOUS

Wallpapers

Wallpapers are made out of paper, plant fiber, silk, cotton, and so on. All of those materials come from renewable sources. There are also some wallpapers made of vinyl or metal foil. Metal foils are lower in emissions, but foils, as well as vinyls, create disposal problems. In addition, vinyl and vinyl coated wallcoverings, if made out of soft plastics, are less stable and may offgas for a long time. Both vinyl and metal foil require manufacturing processes that are highly polluting.

Adhesives can be a problem especially for heavy wallpapers, but there are low-toxic adhesives available. Lighter wallpapers can be applied with light, water-based glue.

Acoustic panels

Acoustic panels, tiles, and acoustic wall coverings are usually made of mineral fibers or fiberglass backing with fabric coverings. They are long-term sources of formaldehyde and other gases, and are highly dust retentive. Because fiber acoustic panels produce volatile emissions, they are known for causing respiratory problems. Still, the acoustical

properties of many interiors may require noise reduction, which can be achieved by ceiling panels made out of wood fibers, tapestries or cork, if the fire rating permits.

Metals

Virtually all metals used in interiors are both very durable and chemically safe, which make them good choices when designing for chemically sensitive people. But metals also represent significant amount of "embodied energy"; their production requires significant amounts of energy, and is often highly polluting. Aluminum has the highest energy content: approximately four times more then steel. Metals can be, in most cases, successfully recycled, employing a fraction of the energy (approximately 10 percent) and saving nonrenewable resources required for new products.

Another concern, when specifying metal furniture, appliances and accessories, is caused by the finishing methods. For example, chrome plating not only uses rare ore, but also produces significant amount of toxic waste.

Glass

Glass is made out of natural resources that are available in abundance. The manufacturing process is much lower in energy requirements than that of metals. Glass is chemically safe, and can be enriched by various finishing methods, for example: sand blasting, or etching, or laminated for safety.

Also, glass can be recycled into a variety of products including floor tiles.

Additional information:

More in-depth analysis can be found:

• Specific information about individual toxics:
Harte, John, Cheryl Holdren, Richard Schneider, and Christine Shirley. *Toxics A to Z: A Guide to Everyday Pollution Hazards.* Berkeley and Los Angeles: University of California Press, 1991.

• Analyses of various materials and products:
"Global choices. Environmental Action and the Design Professional." A Continuing Education Seminar sponsored by The American Society of Interior Designers. At the National Convention, Denver, July 17, 1991.

• Listing of manufacturers and products:
Fuston, Andrew and Kim Plaskon Nadel. "The Green Pages. The Contract Interior Designer's Guide to Environmentally Responsible Products and Materials." Manuscript. New York, Spring 1993.

Schomer, Victoria. "Interior Concerns Resource Guide." Manuscript. Mill Valley, CA, October 1991.

Besides MSDS, some of the manufacturers have done detailed research of their products impact on IAQ and made the findings available on request. For example, the office furniture manufacturer Steelcase Inc. published studies evaluating some of their workstations, chairs, workstation panels, fabrics, coatings, and so on.

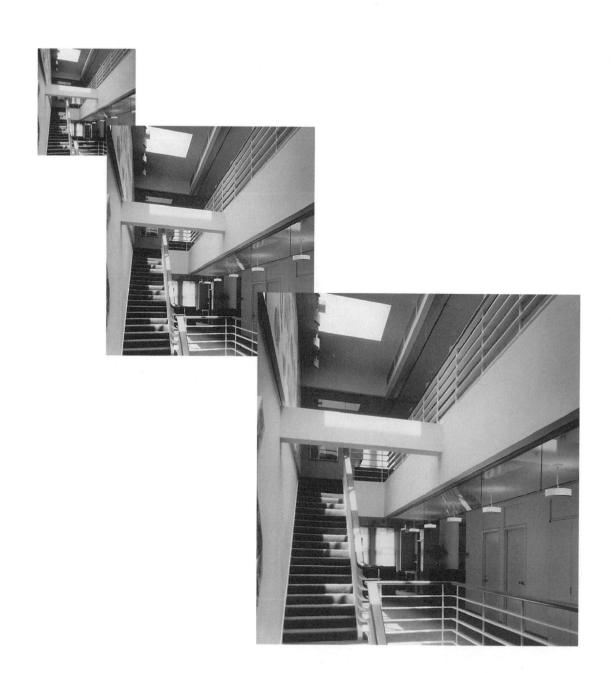

Part III:
Case Studies

Applying environmental methodology to a project is like putting many pieces of a puzzle together. The process requires making the initial effort, planning, acquiring information and organizing all the pieces. It requires a team of professionals working together to resolve various aspects. "It is an interesting and challenging process. I felt like an orchestrator staging experience for other people, initiating human interaction" This is how the process was described to me when I interviewed Stanley Selengut, president and founder of Harmony.

In the four projects described in this part it took a close coordination of the efforts of the developer, client, architect, local power company, research scientist, environmentalist and contractor to implement the ideas. The initial concept may have originated from finding the best solution for the given location (Harmony), from the client's philosophy (NRDC), or from the commitment to the local community (West Bend). Although none of the projects is an example of perfection, and while each makes only a small contribution to alleviating environmental damage, they all are steps in the right direction and they all set the example for future developments.

It is not my intention to compare these examples, but rather to point out their variety. The projects span from a tourist resort, through offices of an insurance or publishing company to a nonprofit environmental organization. The people who were the instrumental forces behind these projects prove that the deciding force may come from any of the parties involved, from all ends of the building process:

corporate world, environmental organization, developer, or environmental consultant. The projects addressed environmental concerns in various degrees. For example, Harmony represents the holistic approach; NRDC focused on energy efficiency and providing healthy environment for people working in a space; at 555 Broadway, the main concern was indoor air quality; for West Bend Mutual the important factor was commitment to the region and their employees.

As skeptics keep challenging the economic benefits of environmentally responsible designs, there are more and more examples that prove that well thought out projects can integrate environmental concerns with economic soundness. The projects described in the following pages are perfect examples of ethics and economy working together. In various degrees, and for various reasons the projects proved to make fiscal sense: Harmony is profitable through its low cost of operation and the appeal it makes to the people choosing it for vacation; NRDC's energy efficiency techniques save operating costs; West Bend's initial cost returned itself in increased productivity.

I would like to express my appreciation to Stanley Selengut, president and founder of Harmony; Asher Derman, of Green October Foundation; Ashok Gupta, Senior Energy Analyst at NRDC; and Robert J. Schmitt, Facilities Manager at West Bend Mutual. Without their help this part of the book would not exist.

The icon image of the stairway used throughout Part III is courtesy of NRDC.

CHAPTER 6
HARMONY
A Center for the Study of Sustainable Resort Development

Harmony, a tourist resort that opened October 24th, 1993 on St. John, U.S. Virgin Islands, is dedicated to the principles of sustainable development. It has been singled out by the U.S. National Park Service as a model for future developments inside national parks. The resort is an example of the holistic approach, which addresses the multiple layers of impact that every development has on the environment. The methods used while building, the choices of materials and products, the future demands of support and maintenance, all respect an existing ecosystem. It is also important that the resort was developed in cooperation with both local

Fig. III-1:
The view of Maho Bay with one of the resort's units.
(Photo: courtesy of Maho Bay Camps.)

government and the community, and future activities at Harmony will focus on education and information, as well as the promotion of the region's culture and traditions. Harmony also functions as a "living laboratory" for studies of the performance of renewable energy systems and as an information center for sustainable development.

The project is the result of the joint effort of the owner and developer Stanley Selengut; New York based architect James Hadley; the Virgin Islands Energy Office (VIEO); and the Virgin Islands National Park of the National Park Service. Technical assistance and consultation to the project were provided by Sandia National Laboratories through the VIEO.

The resort consists of 8 guest houses (32 are planned) and is located within the boundaries of the Virgin Islands National Park, in a remote corner of St. John in the U.S. Virgin Islands. Harmony is a part of the larger Maho Bay Camps complex, which includes Maho Bay Campground and Estate Concordia. All of them were developed with the environment in mind, and through social appeal and energy and water saving technologies have proven to be profitable as well. "The goal of Harmony is to demonstrate that an ecotourism facility can balance both nature and culture–can, in fact, be mutually enhancing," says Stanley Selengut, developer, owner, operator and mastermind behind this project.

Since the hillside on which the resort is located is erosion-prone, all houses were built in the existing spaces between large trees. The buildings were designed with a small footprint and are connected with elevated boardwalks, so as not to disturb local plants. The scale of the structures also minimizes their visual impact on surrounding park. During the construction, special attention was given to avoiding

damage to the existing vegetation; construction access followed future circulation routes and all construction vehicles movement was programmed.

A typical unit consists of a three-bedroom, two-story home. The buildings and interior spaces are designed to maximize comfort with the least amount of energy used. The complex utilizes passive solar energy concepts, including landscape shading, overhangs and reflective glass panels in all windows. Additional climate control is provided by wind scoops, cross-ventilation and ceiling fans. The energy needed for ceiling fans, refrigerators, microwaves and all other standard appliances is generated

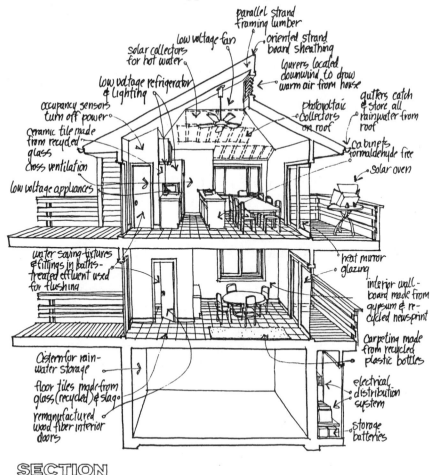

parallel strand framing lumber

low voltage fan

solar collectors for hot water

oriented strand board sheathing

louvers located downwind to draw warm air from house

low voltage refrigerator & lighting

occupancy sensors turn off power

photovoltaic collectors on roof

gutters catch & store all rainwater from roof

ceramic tile made from recycled glass

cross ventilation

cabinets formaldehyde free

solar oven

low voltage appliances

water saving fixtures & fittings in baths- treated effluent used for flushing

heat mirror glazing

interior wall-board made from gypsum & recycled newsprint

carpeting made from recycled plastic bottles

cistern for rain-water storage

floor tiles made from glass (recycled) & slag

remanufactured wood fiber interior doors

electrical distribution system

storage batteries

SECTION

Fig. III-2:
Section through one of the units.

(Drawing: J. Hadley.)

by sun or wind, so the whole resort is "off the grid." Energy for every unit is provided by an 1100-watt photovoltaic array of panels located on the roof of the buildings and is stored in underground batteries. Backup power is generated by a 1.5 kilowatt wind turbine built on a nearby hill. All lighting and appliances are energy-efficient, and operate on timers and occupancy sensors. Passive solar thermal energy is also used to heat water, make ice, and cook food in an outdoor oven. Using renewable energy sources lowered operating costs of the resort, prevented the high costs associated with bringing electric power from outside, and lessened intrusion into the park's landscape. Similarly, the resort is self-sufficient in providing guests with water. Rainwater is collected in cisterns for drinking and washing; waste water is treated and recycled for irrigation and toilet flushing. Water-saving fixtures limit water consumption. Organic waste is composted into garden mulch. A computer terminal in every house monitors and informs guests about outside weather conditions and energy use. Through the terminal guests can also access detailed information on materials, products and technologies used at the resort. Guests can also input comments, which are sent back to the management.

Harmony is built from local or recycled materials without sacrificing the aesthetics. Insulation and wallboard are made from recycled newsprint. Quarry floor tiles are made from recycled clay and scraps, ceramic tile in the bathrooms from recycled glass. All furniture, except beds, are either second-hand or built out of recycled materials. Bed sheets and upholstery for chairs are made of solid, unbleached, undyed, organically grown, naturally colored cotton, colorful throw rugs out of recycled plastic, doormats from ground-up tires. White interior walls are decorated with artifacts from tribal

communities of South America tagged with information labels encouraging support of indigenous art. The furnishing concept is complemented by such details as: recycled toilet paper, biodegradable soaps and cleaning products, and recycling bins with can and glass crushers. All the building materials and appliances used in Harmony are available commercially.

Another interesting and valuable side of the Harmony project is the resort's educational and research aspect. Not only does Harmony expose guests and visitors to "off the grid" living, and to environmentally responsible products and life style, but it also functions as a testing laboratory for new technologies and products. In addition the resort offers education on sustainable technologies to local children and citizens.

Fig. III-3:
Typical interior.
(Photo: courtesy of Maho Bay Camps.)

CHAPTER 7
555 BROADWAY
New York, NY
by Asher Derman, Ph.D.,
Project Consultant.

The benefits of green building techniques are considered to be: the improved health of workers, office personnel or home owners; productivity gains in the workplace; reductions in the use of building products that contain hazardous or toxic materials; energy efficient lighting, equipment and windows, which reduce the fossil fuel required for energy production and result in reductions in air pollution and global warming; the reduction or elimination of the use of ozone depleting CFCs in furniture manufacture, refrigeration, or products; reduction in the amount of waste produced because of better (or green) purchasing policies, which in turn, decrease the demands on natural resources; and, increases in building material (or component) longevity, and the ease of building maintenance, repair, or material reuse. All of these environmental benefits are sought as additions to the vocabulary of new building specification or as the new elements of renovated buildings.

Office installations such as the NRDC, EDF, and Audubon Society represent key examples of what can be achieved using green building techniques, but they do not necessarily represent the range of problems encountered in projects attempting to use the green building vocabulary.

Just a few blocks south of the Audubon Society a major publisher has taken space in a landmarked, 100 year old building to house over 700 employees. The publisher began with an extensive green agenda, became involved with issues representing their unique encounter with program vs. aesthetics vs.

costs, and, in the end, realized some remarkable achievements for its staff.

Energy conservation measures related to the building's shell were high on the list of program requirements and were achieved primarily through the use of insulation and window replacements. Air-Krete, a first choice foamed-in-place benign insulation material, was replaced (because of cost) by rigid fiberglass board (a formaldehyde emitting material, but with a stabilized fiberglass fiber). Almost 200 double hung windows were rebuilt and reglazed, but not with the first choice energy conserving Southwall Heat Mirror double pane glass. Instead, because the New York City Landmarks Commission believed Heat Mirror glass would diminish the historic character of the building's main facade, a less energy efficient clear double pane insulating glass was used. Then, in order to deal with the uncontrolled impact of sunshine through half of the windows, operable Mecco Shades needed to be installed. Still, daylight entering the windows from all exposures helps provide an energy reduction and an illumination benefit for approximately 40% of all offices and workstations.

The issue of indoor air quality was also a paramount concern; particularly in the context of furniture selections and surface finishing choices. Requests were made of all furniture manufacturers invited to bid on the project for information describing the levels of VOCs, formaldehyde, and particulate matter that would be emitted by their products. Information of this type, created through independent scientific analysis, has been carried by major manufacturers beginning since 1992. In addition, Material Safety Data Sheets (MSDS) describing the chemical components of all other building products were also requested from vendors. With such a body of information in hand, informed

(but not scientific) decisions could be made regarding which furniture and building products might leave the least chemical imprint on the building's indoor air quality. However, as with all decisions, environmental concerns represented only one of many factors that contributed to final selections.

Initially, Technion "TOS II" systems furniture was selected for open workstations and Kimball "Footprint" furniture for free standing enclosed offices. But, as a result of bottom line negotiations, Technion "Descor" furniture was also selected for the enclosed offices. Company test data for Technion work surfaces indicated acceptable, but unusually enduring levels of formaldehyde offgassing. Close inspection of mock-ups revealed that the underside of the work surfaces were not finished or sealed and thus contributed to the formaldehyde levels. On request, all exposed particle board surfaces were closed with sealer.

Carpet covers approximately 100,000 square feet of space. Wool was the first choice, but became too costly, and gave way to a less costly DuPont nylon product. In the end, select areas used wool, other areas nylon. From an air quality point of view, the carpet was specified with jute (vs. synthetic) backing and either tacked or adhered, when necessary, with a water-based low VOC adhesive. Based on manufacturer's literature and MSDSs, other decisions about wall paints, enamels, adhesives, and linoleum flooring were also implemented to reduce the potential chemical impact on indoor air quality.

Theory, in many instances, was followed by the practice of selecting low VOC and formaldehyde emitting materials and products. Uniquely, the theory was also tested by pre- and post-occupancy air quality tests for thirty VOCs and formaldehyde. As predicted, initial pre-occupancy VOC and formaldehyde emissions were detected, but at levels below those regulated by government standards. Post-occupancy air quality tests taken two months later, at the same sites, indicated even lower VOC and formaldehyde levels. The offices, in terms of theory and application, were a chemical indoor air quality success.

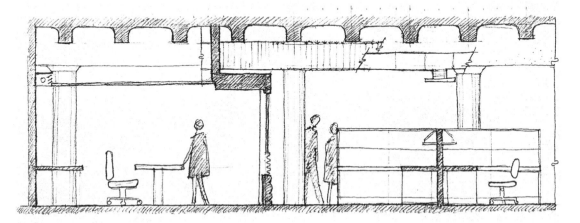

However, important caveats should be kept in mind. Recent studies have identified the major sources of building indoor air pollution to be (in rank order): fungi, mold and mildew; dusts; low or high relative humidity; bacteria; formaldehyde; fibrous glass; carbon monoxide; VOCs; tobacco smoke; and ozone. Simply stated, the best of green design and specification will only be as good as initial decisions, and the equally important, subsequent building and workplace programs that maintain the facility.

Fig. III-4:
Section through typical office.
(Drawing: A. Derman.)

CHAPTER 8
NRDC HEADQUARTERS
New York, NY

The Natural Resources Defense Council (NRDC) is a national organization dedicated to protecting public health and providing conservation of land and natural resources. Completed in 1989, NRDC's New York headquarters became a benchmark of energy efficiency for commercial office renovation. The office is located in a prewar loft building at 40 West 20th Street. The energy efficiency was achieved by interlocking a variety of environmentally responsible decisions in the design of the offices. The project architect, Croxton Collaborative, a leading "green architecture" firm based in New York, used a number of strategies, including maximizing the use of daylight and providing lighting systems based on task/ambient approach.

Fig. III-5:
The NRDC's interior staircase.
(Photo: Mallory Hattie. Courtesy of NRDC.)

The three floors of space were designed to function as a single unit with the natural light, captured through skylights and windows, as the unifying factor. Ribbons of glass around private offices, open-ended hallways and an interior staircase, all help to distribute the light throughout the space. The artificial lighting was designed to provide light only where and when it was needed. The level of ambient light is 25-30 footcandles; the task lighting directed at work surfaces brings the light level to 70-100 footcandles. To further reduce energy consumption and get all the benefit of natural light, the office has a self-monitoring system that responds to the presence of daylight and to an occupant in the space.

Fig. III-6:
One of the perimeter offices at NRDC.
(Photo: Otto Baitz. Courtesy of NRDC.)

Con Edison, the New York City utilities company, followed up the work at NRDC's offices with a one-year study on its energy consumption. Flack + Kurtz' Lighting Design Group conducted the monitoring and issued a report that proved that the

energy efficient lighting designs at NRDC were both environmentally and economically beneficial. "The initial use of energy saving technologies, incorporating T8 fluorescent lamps, electronic ballasts, occupancy sensors, and strategic use of daylighting contribution were the principal factors in reducing the maximum potential demand. As a result, NRDC's 1991 lighting density averaged only 0.40 W/ sq. ft., as compared to a typical commercial tenant lighting density of 2 W/sq.ft.. This resulted in a yearly cost savings of approximately $12,500 or an average of $48.00 saved per day, when compared to a typical commercial tenant" ("Consolidated Edison Co....," p.6).

Among the other strategies, the design conserves energy through the installation of an HVAC system that uses outdoor air below 55° F to cool the offices during the fall, winter and spring. The insulation used was two-and-a-half times more efficient then the typical insulation used in standard commercial buildings, raising the thermal resistance of the walls and roof. In addition, the double-glazed windows and skylights, with a thermal break in the frames, reduce heat loss in the winter and heat gain in the summer.

Energy savings were not the only environmental concern. To provide occupants with fresh air and to lower the level of pollutants, the air is changed 8 to 15 times an hour, instead of 4 to 5 times as in an average office. Formaldehyde-free wool and nylon carpets were installed with natural jute backing and jute-and-hair pads. All paints used in the office were latex, and all chipboard used for the furniture was sealed to limit offgassing. In many cases the offices were furnished with recycled furniture, which not only underscores NRDC's commitment to "green" interiors but also makes the office feel homey.

Nobody at NRDC measured the savings in reduced absenteeism and increased productivity, but people working in this office appreciate the effects of thoughtful design. It is clearly visible in "the staff's enthusiastic reception of the energy-saving techniques, and the resulting hospitable environment that connects its inhabitants visually to the city around them. Natural light is less noted as an energy saving device and more as the welcomed presence of the sun–the Earth's great clock. As one employee assessed it: 'It makes me feel good to work here knowing that we're saving energy. Most people would think that an environmentally designed office wouldn't be comfortable, but here the colors are warm and restful, and the sunlight is welcomed' " (Crosbie, p.89).

CHAPTER 9
WEST BEND MUTUAL INSURANCE COMPANY
West Bend, WI

West Bend Mutual Insurance Company's new 150,000-square foot headquarters building in West Bend, WI, winner of the 1992 Intellex Building for Excellence Award, may be a major step toward answering the challenge set by skeptics to prove the economic benefits of environmentally responsible design. An independent study conducted by the Center for Services Research and Education at Rensselaer Polytechnic Institute, Troy, NY, demonstrated that the integrated mechanical and electrical systems tied together through a sophisticated automation system within the building not only improved occupant comfort, but also led to a productivity increase that paid for the systems in less than one year.

Fig. III-7:
West Bend Mutual Insurance Co.
new headquarters building in West
Bend, WI

(Photo: Courtesy of Edward J. Purcell)

The building was designed by the Zimmerman Design Group, an architectural firm from Wauwatosa. The project architect, David Drews, wanted the new headquarters to blend in with the wooded rural Wisconsin landscape. The building is set back from the road, with the front entrance shrouded by trees. The exterior of locally quarried domolite limestone and sand-colored brick, the fragmented massing, the central tower and the gabled roofs of the building relate to traditional architecture of the region. Surrounding the building are 60 acres of grasses and wild flowers, as well as more than 700 trees; in the future, the property will be enlarged by additional 100 acres.

The most significant improvement in providing comfort for the employees was achieved through the installation of Personal Environment Modules (PEMs), also known as Environmentally Responsive Workstations (ERWs). The stations were designed

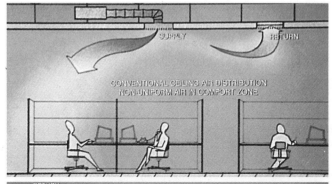

Fig. III-8:
Air distribution throughout the space with conventional systems.

(Drawing: courtesy of Johnson Controls.)

Fig. III-9:
Air distribution with Personal Environments.

(Drawing: courtesy of Johnson Controls.)

by Johnson Controls in Milwaukee. Through the use of slide controls located on a panel at their desks, occupants can individually control temperature and airflow within their own spaces through vents and radiant heaters built into their furniture. Despite open-office design, the stations also provide direct control of task lighting and allow users to set white noise. A motion sensor automatically turns off the systems within the space if the occupant leaves, and brings them back on when he or she returns, contributing to overall energy efficiency. The technical benefits of the workstations are complemented by ergonomically designed furniture. "During the independent study, ERWs were turned off randomly throughout the building to measure their effect on productivity. [During those days] the building manager was inundated with phone calls from angry staff, some of whom threatened to take the day off if the units were not brought back on line" (Beck, p.34).

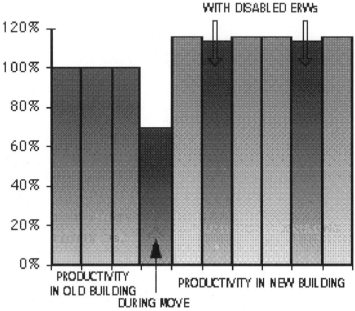

Fig. III-10:
Productivity change over time at West Bend Mutual.

(Source: Beck, p.35.)

A team of researchers at Rensselaer Polytechnic Institute has shown a direct, measurable link between architectural design, individual comfort control, and productivity. The one-year study, headed by Professor Walter Kroner, measured productivity prior to the move, during the transition from the old facility to the new, and in the new building. According to the study, productivity shot up 16 percent because of the overall combined effects of the new facility. During the time when ERWs were turned off productivity dropped 2 percent, proving the direct impact the stations have on office productivity. "Based on the company's annual salary base of $13 million ... the productivity increases from the ERWs alone resulted in an annual savings of $260,000. The system paid for itself in less than one year" (Beck, p.35).

Conclusion

John Picard, Principal of Environmental Enterprises, Los Angeles, addressed a panel of interior designers and architects at Green October '93 with these words: "You are a powerful group and powerfully gifted individuals. You're connected in a powerful profession rooted in change. This is where we must start: together. Sitting Bull said: let's put our minds together and see what we can make for our children. He didn't say, let's put our minds together and see what we could make for our stockholders. Or let's see what we can make for our clients. Chief Warren Line says that we will never have peace as long as we fight Mother Earth. This is a peace we must create because that is where our life is. No more short-term decisions and paybacks. We must make long-term decisions with compassion for our future. One person can make the difference" ("Green October...," p.54.).

Environmentally conscious design is a way of thinking. It is a methodology of approaching all aspects of design and taking responsibility for all decisions. Paul Bierman-Lytle, one of the architects involved in the "green" design movement, is concerned that just as architects in the 1970s focused almost exclusively on energy issues, today's designers tackle indoor air pollution with blinders on. "They don't see that it's part of a much bigger issue: esthetics, energy sustainability, and the health of the occupant, the craftsmen and the planet" (Dana, "Renaissance...," p.65). The objective of environmentally conscious design is not only to save energy

or achieve clean indoor air, but to look at environmental quality in a holistic sense throughout the whole design process.

Resolving any one of the issues doesn't make the design environmentally conscious. All of the aspects have to be analyzed; the goal is to achieve design that is as balanced with the environment's and inhabitants' needs as possible. Sometimes difficult choices have to be made. A given project may require the use of more energy, or the avoidance of certain materials for the benefit of particular group of occupants (elderly, children, etc.). Interior designers have to remember what is defined by the ASID as their responsibility: "To enhance the quality of life and protect the health, safety, and welfare of the public," and make knowledgeable decisions.

All design professionals, including interior designers, architects, advertising designers, product and fashion designers, have to be aware of unintended as well as intended consequences of their designs, consequences that take an active role in forming people's ethical and aesthetic needs and expectations. This is by no means a trivial responsibility.

Professional ethics and the new aesthetic demand that we, as designers, go beyond what is immediately visible. "Design that makes us sick or that destroys the earth is not beautiful" (Dana, "Greening…," p.80). As more "healthy" buildings and interiors are designed, and as the specifications of materials and methods become more responsible, it will be more economical to build, since the industry will have to respond to the increased market and competition. The demand for such architecture and interiors will grow as the "healthy" choices of products and materials increase. This is called in ecology the "positive feedback loop": self-accelerating change. Also, as more responsible, voluntary action is taken by the

design community, by the industry and by the public, the unnecessary overgrowth of regulations and laws may be avoided.

The crucial issue today is to learn how to use the Earth's capital–the natural resources of air, soil and water–in a sustainable manner. To secure a better world tomorrow, education is needed. The knowledge is available. Now designers have to learn how to apply ideas of sustainability: how to utilize resources without destroying the future. It is important that this book be seen only as an introduction that points out the main issues involved; it is every designer's responsibility to seek further information and to update it constantly with his/her own research.

If the change is going to take place, it has to start in schools, with the new generation of future interior designers. In the previous decade or so, ecological studies have been incorporated into many school programs, but they are often treated as a separate subject, not connected them with other professional knowledge. It is now necessary to bring to students the understanding of how the environment and its functioning is impacted by human activities, so that they can make knowledgeable decisions later. "Even if the…corporate greed of many design offices makes [socially responsible] design impossible, students should at least be encouraged to work in this manner. For showing students new areas of engagement, we may set up alternate patterns of thinking about design problems. We may help them to develop the kind of social and moral responsibility that is needed in design" (Papanek, p.58). In the ongoing process of redefining the interior design profession, it is very important that environmental concerns receive appropriate attention.

As it was pointed many times in this book, to achieve sustainable and healthy indoor spaces, it is

necessary that interior designers work in a team with architects, mechanical and structural engineers, environmental consultants, lighting consultants, acoustical consultants, landscape designers and contractors. The experienced builders of environmentally conscious spaces often prize manufacturers of "green" products as an invaluable resource. The future occupants and maintenance personnel are also important partners in the process. Only multi-professional interaction can insure successful completion of such a complex undertaking as building spaces that will have a positive influence on the well-being of the people and that will not compromise the global environment.

It is late and a lot of damage has been done to the environment, but it is not too late, if we will begin to act today.

Part IV:
Existing Resources

The listings below are not complete. They are, rather, just samplers of vast resources available.

LEGISLATION

Environmentally responsible design is no longer just a matter of ethics and conscience. More and more, care for the environment is being mandated by law. Legislation is formed on national, state or city levels. Listed below are only the highlights, but they should give a sense of the complexity of the effort to protect the environment.

Information listed below is based on US EPA materials and Jon Naar listings (Naar, pp. 231-244).

The National Environmental Policy Act of 1969 (NEPA)

Signed in 1970 and sometimes called the Magna Carta of environmental legislation, NEPA requires federal agencies to take into account the environmental consequences of all their plans and activities.

Pollution prevention

• The Clean Air Act (CAA)

First enacted in 1955, finally signed in 1970, the Clean Air Act is the environmental law par excellence. At the heart of the CAA are National Ambient Air-Quality Standards (NAAQS), which establish maximum allowable concentrations for the

pollutants that the EPA deems to be particularly widespread and dangerous. Although the EPA sets these nationally applicable air-quality standards, it is up to the states to meet them. The act also imposes various performance standards on factories, power plants, and other so-called "stationary sources" of air pollution, as well as on automobile emissions.

• The Clean Air Act Amendment of 1990

This amendment, which includes a list of 189 air pollutants to be regulated, is affecting furniture manufacturers, primarily in the finishing areas. Both the status of the air quality where a particular manufacturing facility is located and the quantity of VOCs emitted by the plant are determining factors of whether the facility will fall under governmental regulation. Currently, the EPA is reviewing technology for reducing VOC emissions. To assist the EPA in its review and in its development of specific requirements for wood furniture manufacturers, a Joint Industry Steering Committee has been formed by The American Furniture Manufacturers Association (AFMA), the Kitchen Cabinet Manufacturers Association (KCMA), the Business and Institutional Furniture Manufacturers Association (BIFMA) and the National Paint and Coatings Association (NPCA).

• The Clean Water Act (CWA)

Signed in 1972, the CWA addressed two main issues: municipal sewage and industrial discharges. All municipal waste has to be treated before being discharged into waterways, and all facilities discharging into waters have to obtain a permit. Every facility is responsible for monitoring its discharges.

• The Safe Drinking Water Act (SDWA)

Adopted in 1974 and substantially amended in

1986, the SDWA requires the EPA to set standards for contaminants in public drinking water supplies. The SDWA takes steps toward the protection of underground drinking water supplies.

• The Resource Conservation and Recovery Act (RCRA)

The RCRA addresses the disposal of solid waste, primarily regulating landfills, but leaving most of the problems to state and local governments. The EPA developed a list of hazardous wastes and established a regulatory scheme for their handling and disposal.

• The Toxic Substances Control Act (TSCA)

This act seeks to develop information about toxic substances. It requires manufacturers to notify the EPA before they begin to produce a new chemical substance. The EPA may restrict or forbid the use of any substance if the agency has a reasonable basis to conclude that there is a risk of injury to health or the environment.

• The Federal Insecticide, Fungicide, and Rodenticide Act (FIFRA)

The FIFRA regulates the registration, marketing, and use of pesticides.

Wildlife and habitat protection

• The Endangered Species Act

This act, signed in 1973, is based on congressional recognition that endangered species of wildlife and plants "are of aesthetic, ecological, educational, historical, recreational, and scientific value to the Nation and its people."

• The Marine Mammal Protection Act

This act is intended to protect, conserve, and encourage research on marine animals. The basic idea is that marine mammals are off limits, with the exceptions of, for example, subsistence hunting.

• The Marine Protection, Research, and Sanctuaries Act

This act, known as the Ocean Dumping Act, regulates the dumping of material in US waters to protect the marine environment.

Energy-related legislation

• The National Energy Policy Act of 1992

This act is commonly referred to as EPACT (Energy Policy Act) and was signed into law by President Bush in October 1992. This law aims to reduce energy consumption through more competitive electricity generation and conservation initiatives. EPACT touches every aspect of energy policy in the USA, including resources, consumption, conservation, utility incentives, IRS tax exclusions for rebates, renewable energy fuels, vehicle fuels and product efficiency standards applicable to motors, distribution transformers and lamps. It mandates minimum efficacy and color rendering standards in the manufacture of popular fluorescent and incandescent reflector lamp types commonly used in industrial and commercial applications. This legislation affects general service F40 four-foot medium bi-pin, two-foot U-bent, F96T12 and F96T12/HO eight-foot fluorescent lamp types. Incandescent lamp types affected are reflector lamps of medium screw base design with diameters larger than 2.75 inches, voltages of 115-130 volts and wattage ranges from 40 to 205 watts.

• **The Public Utility Regulatory Policies Act (PURPA)**

The PURPA encourages the development of renewable energy and small-scale power production.

• **The National Appliance Energy Conservation Act**

Signed in 1987, this act sets minimum-efficiency standards for new-home heating and cooling systems, refrigerators, freezers, small gas furnaces, and other appliances.

Other legislation

• **The Customs & Trade Act**

Enacted in 1990, this act addresses imports of goods and materials in relation to the source country's respect for internationally recognized human rights; policies against trade and production of narcotics; martial law; transferring power to a civilian government. If these conditions are not met, the act directs the President to impose political or economic sanctions that he considers appropriate.

• **Proposition 65**

California's Safe Drinking Water and Toxics Enforcement Act, which went into effect in February 1988, is a good example of a state initiative resulting from public demand. The initiative was passed overwhelmingly despite a multimillion dollar campaign against it by industry and the governor. Under this law, no business may expose people to chemicals that cause cancer or reproductive problems such as birth defects, sterility, or miscarriage without giving "clear and reasonable warning." Failure to give warning can bring fines of up to $2,500 a day for each exposure.

Pending legislation

• The Indoor Air Quality Act of 1993

Passed in the Senate in October 1993, this proposal, sponsored by Senators Mitchell (D-ME), Charee (R-RI) and Lautenberg (D-NJ), requires numerous IAQ research and risk management activities such as Federal and private research, management practices guidance/training, assessment of and recommendations for ventilation standards, contaminant health advisories, a national IAQ response plan, Federal and other building demonstration program, a state grant program, and an IAQ Clearinghouse.

Referred to Energy and Commerce; Education and Labor; Science, Space and Technology in April 1993 by Senator Kennedy (D-MA), the Act requires numerous IAQ research activities, including: Federal research, technology demonstration program, modes IAQ training course, contaminant health advisories, IAQ clearinghouse, assessment of ventilation standards and guidelines, a national response strategy, assessment of IAQ and corrective actions, state grants.

• The Indoor Air Act of 1993

Introduced in August 1993 by Senator Kennedy (D-MA), it requires the EPA to establish guidelines for identifying and preventing indoor air hazards in new and existing buildings; training and certification of IAQ contractors; national education campaign including health advisories with Action Levels, technology bulletins; clearinghouse; Federal buildings program; State grants; research and other studies.

• Other pending legislation

The Global Warming Prevention Act
The Tropical Forest Protection Act
The Tropical Forestry Initiative Act
The National Energy Policy Act
The Global Climate Change Prevention Act

CERTIFICATION INITIATIVES

Some private groups in the USA have turned to independent "eco-labeling" as a way of ensuring the veracity of environmental claims.

• Air Cleaner Certification Program
Association of Home Appliance Manufacturers
20 N. Wacker Dr.
Chicago, IL 60606
(312)984-5800

• Green Seal,
1733 Connecticut Ave., NW
Washington, DC 20009
(202)328-8095
Green Seal, a nonprofit organization, examines the environmental impact of products and their packaging, from manufacturing through use and disposal.

• IAQ Carpet Testing Program
Carpet and Rug Institute
P.O.Box 2048
Dalton, GA 30722
(800)822-8846

• **Institute for Sustainable Forestry**
P.O. Box 1580
Redway, CA 95560
(707)923-4719
In addition to publishing a newsletter, which promotes sustainable forestry, the Institute has a program for certifying and labeling ecologically harvested forest products.

• **Rainforest Alliance**
SmartWood Program, Suite 512
270 Lafayette St.
New York, NY 10012
(212)941-1900
The Alliance conducts a certification program for sustainable forestry.

• **Scientific Certification Systems**
(previously Green Cross Certification)
1611 Telegraph Ave., Suite 1111
Oakland, CA 94612-2113
(800)829-1416
(510)832-1415
This group operates the Green Cross certification program, which provides third-party verification of the environmental claims of consumer products, ranging from paper products to bed pillows, to hoses and watering systems to cleaning products.

ORGANIZATIONS AND CENTERS

US Government

• **US Environmental Protection Agency**
401 M St., SW
Washington, DC 20460
(800)424-9346
in Washington, DC, 382-3000
The Agency is a federal government agency mandated to protect human health and the environment. It provides information on a variety of environmental concerns, including recycling. A complete listing of state recycling offices is available from the EPA Office of Solid Waste or in their booklet "Recycling Works!" (EPA/530-SW-89-014), which is available on request.

Some of the Regional Offices:
–Region 1
New England
JFK Federal Building
Boston, MA 02203
(617)565-3715
–Region 2
New York, New Jersey, Puerto Rico,
Virgin Islands
26 Federal Plaza
New York, NY 10007
(212)264-2525
–Region 3
Delaware, Maryland, Pennsylvania, Virginia,
West Virginia, District of Columbia
Curtis Building
6th and Walnut
Philadelphia, PA 19106
(215)597-9800

• National Institute for Occupational Safety and Health

944 Chestnut Ridge Rd.
Morgantown, WV 26505
(304)291-4474

The Institute conducts research, recommends standards to the US Department of Labor, and conducts training on various issues. It also undertakes investigations at the request of employees, employers, other federal agencies, and state and local agencies to identify and mitigate workplace problems.

Other organizations and centers

• Center for the Biology of Natural Systems

Queens College
Flushing, NY 11367
(718)670-4180.

The Center conducts research studies on municipal solid waste disposal, renewable energy, and other environmental subjects.

• Council on Economic Priorities

30 Irving Place
New York, NY 10003
(212)420-1133

The Council is a corporate environmental information center. Since 1969, CEP has monitored and analyzed corporate social behavior, producing such guides as *Rating America's Social Conscience* and *Shopping for a Better World*. CEP's Corporate Environmental Clearinghouse publishes many company-specific environmental reports, the single best source for in-depth information in this area.

• **Environmental Action Coalition**
625 Broadway
New York, NY 10012
(212)677-1601
The Coalition is an independent group that works with the New York City Department of Sanitation to organize recycling of newspapers, glass, tin cans, and plastic containers.

• **Environmental Defense Fund**
257 Park Ave. South
New York, NY 10010
(212)505-2100
The Fund is a national nonprofit organization founded nearly 25 years ago that combines scientific research with legal action on a wide range of subjects including recycling, radon, toxic waste and global warming. Through its environmental information exchange the EDF helps state-level groups find technical, scientific and legal information. To find innovative and lasting solutions to environmental problems, the organization publishes literature on such topics as toxic waste, water pollution and recycling.

• **INFORM**
381 Park Ave. South
New York, NY 10016
(212)689-4040
INFORM does research on garbage, toxic waste, water pollution and other environmental topics.

• **Institute for Local Self-Reliance**
2425 18th St., NW
Washington, DC 20009
(202)232-4108
The Institute helps cities and community developers make new products from recycled materials

and provides consultation for solid waste management.

• Natural Resources Defense Council
40 West 20th St.
New York, NY 10011
(212)727-2700

The Council has its offices in Washington, DC, San Francisco, Los Angeles, Honolulu and New York. It is a nonprofit organization that since 1970, has gathered scientists and lawyers working to protect America's natural resources and to improve the quality of the human environment. It combines research, education, advocacy and litigation on toxic substances, air and water pollution, nuclear safety and other subjects. The NRDC pursues these goals through shaping government action at the federal, state and local levels and through extensive public education and outreach.

• National Toxins Campaign
1168 Commonwealth Ave.
Boston, MA 02134
(617)232-4014

The Campaign is working to implement citizen-based preventive solutions to the environmental crisis. The NTC is building a national base of active individuals to move industry and agriculture away from toxin-based production over the next decade. The NTC also provides organizing assistance, technical and legal help, leadership training and environmental testing to grassroots groups.

Organizations devoted to specific issues

• **Air Quality**
–American Society of Heating,
Refrigeration and Air-Handling Engineers
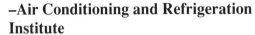
    1791 Tullie Circle NE
    Atlanta, GA 30329
    (404)636-8400

–Air Conditioning and Refrigeration
Institute
    1501 Wilson Blvd., 6th floor
    Arlington, VA 22209
    (703)524-8800

–Association of Home Appliance
Manufacturers, Air Cleaner Certification
Program
    20 N. Wacker Dr.
    Chicago, IL 60606
    (312)984-5800

–Coalition for Clean Air
    122 Lincoln Blvd., Suite 201
    Venice, CA 90291
    (213)450-3190

–Indoor Air Information Service
    P.O.Box 8446
    Santa Cruz, CA 95061
    (408)425-3946

–EPA–Indoor Air Division
    Mail Code ANR-445
    401 M St., NW
    Washington, DC 20210
    (202)382-7400

• Recycling
–National Solid Wastes Management
Association
    1730 Rhode Island Ave., NW
    Washington, DC 20036
    (202)659-4613

–National Recycling Coalition
    1718 M St., NW, Suite 294
    Washington, DC 20036
    (202)625-6408

• Wood
–Rainforest Action Network
    450 Sansome St., Suite 700
    San Francisco, CA 94111
    (415)398-4404
    The Network offers "Wood Users Guide," listing uses of tropical timber, alternatives, sources of wood, information on importers.

–Rainforest Alliance
    270 Lafayette St., Suite 512
    New York, NY 10012
    (212)941-1900
    The Alliance operates the Smart Wood program to certify that wood comes from sustained yield harvests and provides source lists of certified lumber suppliers and wholesale and retail furniture suppliers whose products are made exclusively of Smart Wood.

–Woodworkers Alliance for Rainforest
Protection
    Box 133
    Coos Bay, OR 97420
    (503)269-6907

The Alliance provides information on environmentally responsible sources of wood for wood users, architects, carpenters, fine furniture makers and
instrument makers. They caution that lists easily
become outdated and don't necessarily mean that
every kind of wood from every supplier is from a
certified source; they urge consumers to ask questions.

• Furniture
–American Furniture Manufacturers
Association
    P.O.Box HP-7
    High Point, NC 27261
    (919)884-5000

–American Society of Furniture Designers
    P.O.Box 2688
    521 S. Hamilton St.
    High Point, NC 27261
    (919)884-4074

–Business and Institutional Furniture
Manufacturers Association
    2335 Burton, SE
    Grand Rapids, MI 49506
    (616)243-1681

–Contract Furnishing Council
    1190 The Merchandise Mart
    Chicago, IL 60654
    (312)321-0563

• Energy efficiency resource and
information centers
    In New York, a good source of information is
provided by the Con Edison Conservation Center, in
the Chrysler Building, 42nd Street and Lexington

Avenue. In Queens a similar center is located at 118-29 Queens Boulevard (at Union Turnpike). In New York you can also get answers from Con Edison to energy conservation questions by calling their toll free Enlightened Energy GuideLine: (800)343-4646.

On the West Coast, in San Francisco, The Pacific Gas & Electric Company built a hands-on, state-of-the-art, energy education center, where the design community, as well as the general public, can learn about the impact of their technology choices on a building's energy profile.

Other facilities in the country raise awareness of energy efficiency in such disciplines as lighting or air conditioning.

PUBLICATIONS

Buzzworm. The Environmental Journal, bi-monthly
P.O.Box 6853
Syracuse, NY 13217

DesignSpirit, quarterly
438 Third St.
Brooklyn, NY 11215

E Magazine, bimonthly
P.O. Box 6667
Syracuse, NY 13217
A publication of the Earth Action Network.

Environmental Resource Guide
American Institute of Architects
1735 New York Ave., NW
Washington, DC 20006
(800)365-2724

A project of the AIA's Committee on the Environment (COTE), this guide is a subscription service that is updated quarterly. Topics range from case studies of sustainable architecture, giving examples of environmentally sensitive practices, and specific materials (including aluminum, tropical woods, particleboard, carpet systems and paint) to more general discussions of wetland preservation and indoor air quality.

Garbage. The Practical Journal for the Environment
Old House Journal Corp.
435 9th St.
Brooklyn, NY 11215

"Green Pages. The Contract Interior Designer's Guide to Environmentally Responsible Products and Materials."
Compiled by Andrew Fuston ((212)779-3365) and Kim Plaskon ((212)964-3332). A product resource guide and listing of manufacturers, consultants, mail order catalogues, etc.

"Guide to Resource Efficient Building Elements"
Center for Resourceful Building Technology
P.O.Box 3866
Missoula, MT 59806
(406)549-7678
The Guide (1992) is a reference to over 100 manufacturers of building products with recycled content or building products that make a more efficient use of natural resources in their manufacuring processes. The Guide also includes also a discussion of the effects of natural resource extraction and approaches to job site waste management.

Interior Concerns Resource Guide
Victoria Schomer
P.O.Box 2386
Mill Valley, CA 94942
(415)389-8049
This is a looseleaf folder guide (1991) to environmentally sensitive and low-toxic alternative products as well as educational information for designing and building safe, ecologically sound homes. The guide is focused on residential design.

Safe Home Digest
24 East Ave.,Suite 1300
New Canaan, CT 06840
The newsletter describes and lists safe residential building products and construction methods.

Seed
27 E. 59th Street
New York, NY 10022
Seed is a newsletter published by the New York Chapter of the Institute of Business Designers' Council on the Environment for professional contract interior designers and architects.

The Source Book for Sustainable Design
Architects for Social Responsibility
248 Franklin St.
Cambridge, MA 02139
This reference book offers a comprehensive look at the interconnected issues regarding sustainability. Each chapter analyzes a separate component of the design and construction of a structure, with a list of suggested products.

List of Abbreviations

AIA	American Institute of Architects.
ANSI	American National Standards Institute.
ASHRAE	American Society of Heating, Refrigeration and Air Conditioning Engineers
ASID	American Society of Interior Designers.
BRI	Building related illness.
BTU	British thermal unit, a measure of the quantity of heat.
CFCs	Chlorofluorocarbons, compounds produced in the manufacture of polystyrene products, main cause of ozone layer depletion.
cfm	Cubic feet per minute, unit of air amount used to evaluate performance of ventilation equipment.
CIAQ	Committee on Indoor Air Quality.
CRI	Carpet and Rug Institute.
EDF	Environmental Defense Fund.
EER	Energy efficiency rating.
EMF	Electromagnetic fields.
EPA	Environmental Protection Agency.
ERWs	Environmentally responsive work stations.
ETS	Environmental tobacco smoke, also called second-hand smoke.
FAO	United Nations Food and Agriculture Organization.
HBI	Healthy Buildings International, Inc.
HCFCs	Hydrofluorocarbons, "ozone safe" CFCs substitute.
HUD	Department of Housing and Urban Development.

HVAC	Heating, ventilating and air conditioning.
IAQ	Indoor air quality.
IBD	Institute of Business Designers.
IDCNY	Interior Design Center in New York.
LD50	Lethal dose 50 percent, one of the characteristics of product or material listed on an MSDS, the dose expressed in milligrams per kilogram of body weight that is lethal to 50 percent of laboratory animals when ingested. The lower the LD50, the more toxic the agent is.
MCS	Multiple chemical sensitivities.
MSDS	Material safety data sheet, used to record chemical handling procedures.
NFRC	National Fenestration Rating Council.
NIOSH	National Institute for Occupational Health and Safety.
NRC	National Research Council.
NRDC	Natural Resources Defense Council.
OSHA	Occupational Health and Safety Act.
PCBs	Polychlorinated biphenyls.
PELs	Permissible exposure limits.
PEMs	Personal environment modules.
RAN	Rainforest Action Network.
SBS	Sick building syndrome.
TLV	Threshold limit value, one of the characteristics of product or material listed on an MSDS, the accepted toxicity threshold for a hazardous material. The lower the TLV, the more toxic the agent is.
TSP	Total suspended particulates.
TVOC	Total volatile organic content, one of the characteristics of product or material listed on an MSDS, the volume of the product that will evaporate over time. The higher the TVOC the more the product adds to indoor pollution.
TWA	Time weighted average, one of the characteristics of product or material listed on an MSDS, the allowable exposure

limit over a working day. The lower the TWA, the more toxic the agent is.

UFAC	Upholstered Furniture Action Council.
VDT	Video display terminal.
VIEO	Virgin Islands Energy Office.
VOCs	Volatile organic compounds.
WEB	World Environmental Business.
WHO	World Health Organization.

Bibliography

"A Dose of Green for Indoor Air Pollution." *Facilities Design and Management.* July 1992: 56-57.

Agran, Larry. *The Cancer Connection and What We Can Do About It.* New York: St. Martin's Press, 1977.

"A Healthy Environment Begins at Home." In: *Smarter Energy for a Better World.* Pacific Energy Center exhibit brochure. San Francisco: PG&E, 1992.

Audubon House: Building the Environmentally Responsible, Energy-Efficient Office. National Audubon Society, Croxton Collaborative, Architects. New York: John Wiley & Sons, Inc., 1994.

Beck, Paul E. "Intelligent Design Passes IQ Test." In: *Building Connections.* A Three-part Series for Architects and Allied Professionals On Design for the Environment. March 4, 1993. AIA. Washington, DC, 1993: 34-38.

Branch, Mark Alden. "The State of Sustainability." *Progressive Architecture.* March 1993: 72-79.

Brown, G. Z., Bruce Haglund, Joel Loveland, John S. Reynolds and M. Susan Ubbelohde. *Insideout.* 2nd ed. New York: John Wiley & Sons, Inc., 1992.

Brown, Lester R. "A Generation of Deficits." In: *State of the World 1986; A Worldwatch Institute Report.* New York: W. W. Norton and Co., 1986: 8-11.

Building Connections. A Three-Part Series for Architects and Allied Professionals on Design for the Environment. January 14, March 4, and April 22. Resource Supplement for Program II: Healthy Buildings and Materials. March 4, 1993. AIA. Washington, DC, 1993.

Cohen, Elaine and Aaron Cohen. *Planning the Electronic Office.* New York: McGraw-Hill Book Company, 1983.

"Cold Facts". Pacific Gas and Electric Company pamphlet. San Francisco. 1991.

"Commonly Used Woods to Avoid." Scientific Certification Systems looseleaf listing.

"Consolidated Edison Co. of New York Inc. Office Lighting Demonstration Project Analysis Report of Natural Resources Defense Council, 40 West 20th Street, New York, NY." Prepared by Flack + Kurtz Consulting Engineers Lighting Design Group. Reference No. 88.26027.00. New York, August 3, 1992.

Crosbie, Michael J. "Practicing What They Preach." *Progressive Architecture.* March 1993: 84-89.

Dana, Amy. "Renaissance Man."*Interiors.* July 1991: 65.
——"Greening Up."*Interiors.* March 1992: 80.
——"An Ounce of Prevention." *Interiors.* June 1991: 111.

"Environment." *1992 Britannica Book of the Year.* Chicago: Encyclopædia Britannica, Inc., 1992: 161-165.

"Environmentally Concerned Businesses." *The ASID Report.* March/April 1992: 19.

Evans, Benjamin, H., AIA. *Daylight in Architecture.* New York: Architectural Record Books. McGraw-Hill Book Company, 1981.

Finding New Ways to Put Old Carpet Back to Work. Brochure. Partnership for Carpet Reclamation. Wilmington: Du Pont, 1993.

Fuston, Andrew and Kim Plaskon Nadel. "The Green Pages. The Contract Interior Designer's Guide to Environmentally Responsible Products and Materials." Manuscript. New York, Spring 1993.

"Global Choices. Environmental Action and the Design Professional." A Continuing Education Seminar sponsored by The American Society of Interior Designers. At the National Convention, Denver, July 17, 1991.

Goldstein, Eric A. and Mark A. Izeman. *The New York Environment Book.* Natural Resources Defense Council. Washington, DC: Islan Press, 1990.

Gore, Al. *Earth in the Balance: Ecology and the Human Spirit.* New York: Houghton Mifflin Company, 1992.

Gordon, Harry T. "The Design of Healthy, Energy Efficient Buildings." In: *Building Connections.* A Three-Part Series for Architects and Allied Professionals on Design for the Environment. January 14, March 4, and April 22. Resource Supplement for Program II: Healthy Buildings and Materials. March 4, 1993. AIA. Washington, DC, 1993: 41-49.

"Green October 93. Panel Discussions." Transcript. Recorded at the Green Design and the Sublime Exhibit. A&D Building. New York, October 13, 1993.

Hammel, Debbie. "Bringing Wood to the Table." *Furniture Design & Manufacturing.* December 1991: 24-32

Harf, James E. *The Politics of Global Resources; Population, Food, Energy, and Environment.* Durham, NC: Duke University Press, 1986.

Harte, John, Cheryl Holdren, Richard Schneider and Christine Shirley. *Toxics A to Z. A Guide to Everyday Pollution Hazards.* Berkeley and Los Angeles: University of California Press, 1991.

"Healthy Buildings and Materials." In: *Building Connections.* A Three-Part Series for Architects and Allied Professionals on Design for the Environment. January 14, March 4, and April 22. Resource Supplement for Program II: Healthy Buildings and Materials. March 4, 1993. AIA. Washington, 1993.

Holdsworth, Bill and Antony Sealey. *Healthy Buildings. A Design Primer for a Living Environment.* Essex: Longman Group UK Ltd., 1992.

"How to Cut Energy Costs in Your Apartment." Con Edison Enlightened Energy pamphlet, August 1992.

King, Anthony. "Tackling Indoor Air Quality in the Work Place–The Power of the Market." *IBD/ NY Seed Newsletter.* Issue 6. Fall, 1992: 6-7.

Lewis, Scott. *The Rainforest Book.* NRDC. New York: Living Planet Press, 1990.

Lyle, John Tillman. *Regenerative Design for Sustainable Development.* New York: John Wiley & Sons, Inc., 1994.

Malino, Emily and Dr. Eileen Lee. "Escape from the Electromagnetic Field." *Contract Design.* April 1991: 74-75.

Mead, Thomas. " The Breakthrough Building." *The New York Observer.* May 18, 1992: 15.

Naar, Jon. *Design for a Livable Planet: How You Can Help Clean Up the Environment.* New York: Harper and Row, 1990.

"Notes on the Greening of Interior Design." *Interior Design.* August 1991: 77-92.

Papanek, Victor. Design for the Real World: Human Ecology and Social Change. New York: Pantheon, 1971.

Pearson, David. *The Natural House Book.* New York: Simon & Schuster, 1989

Ramsey, Charles G. and Harold R. Sleeper. *Architectural Graphic Standards.* 6th ed. New York: John Wiley and Sons, Inc., 1970.

Ramsey, Charles G. and Harold R. Sleeper. *Architectural Graphic Standards. 1993 Cumulative Supplement.* 8th ed. New York: John Wiley and Sons, Inc., 1993.

Robertson, Gray. "Indoor Pollution: Sources, Effects and Mitigation Strategies." In: *Environmental Tobacco Smoke.* Proceedings of the International Symposium at McGill University. 1989. Lexington: Lexington Books, 1990: 333-355.

Schomer, Victoria. "Interior Concerns Resource Guide." Manuscript. Mill Valley, CA. October 1991.

Schumacher, E. F. *Small Is Beautiful. Economics as if People Mattered.* New York: Harper and Row, 1973.

Southwick, Charles H. *Global Ecology.* Sunderland, MA: Sinauer Associates Inc., 1985.

Stark, Judy: "Saving the Rain Forest." *Times Floridian.* July 21, 1992.

"Summit to Save the Earth." *Time*. June 1, 1992: pp. 40-58.

The Language of Lighting. Elk Grove Village, Il: McGraw-Edison Company, Halo Lighting Division, 1983.

The Progressive Review. No. 289. Washington, DC June 1990.

United States Department of the Interiors and National Park Service. *Guiding Principles of Sustainable Design.* Denver Service Center. 1993.

United States Environmental Protection Agency (EPA). 1989. "Report to Congress on Indoor Air Quality, Vol II: Assessment and Control of Indoor Air Pollution." Washington, DC.

United States Environmental Protection Agency (EPA). 1990. "Evaluation of the Potential Carcinogenicity of Electromagnetic Fields, Draft Report." Washington, DC.

United States Environmental Protection Agency (EPA). 1991. "Building Air Quality. A Guide for Building Owners and Facility Managers." Washington, DC.

United States Environmental Protection Agency (EPA). 1991. "Introduction to Indoor Air Quality. A Reference Manual." EPA/400/3-91/003. Washington, DC.

Vale, Brenda and Robert Vale. *The Autonomous House: Design and Planning for Self Sufficiency.* New York: Universe Books, 1975.

Vischer, Jacqueline C. *Environmental Quality in Offices.* New York: Van Nostrand Reinhold, 1989.

Wagner, Michael. "Architects Convene at Earth Summit in Rio." *Architecture.* August 1992: 81-82.

———"Energy Tool." *Interiors.* June 1992: 96.

———"How to Get Green." *Interiors.* July 1992: 72-74.

———"Natural Resources." *Interiors.* March 1993: 59-62.

———"Re-psyched Future." *Interiors.* September 1990: 12.

———"Visionary Architect." *Interiors.* March 1993: 54-59.

Watson, Jacky. *Textiles and the Environment.* London: The Economist Intelligence Unit, 1991.

Wellner, Pamela and Eugene Dickey. *The Wood Users Guide.* San Francisco: Rainforest Action Network, 1991.

"White Son Creates a Warm Welcome." *Lighting Quarterly.* Phillips Lighting Company. Volume 1, No.3, 1992: 1-4

Whitehead, Randall: "Fear of Fluorescents." *The ASID Report.* March/April 1992: 15.

Wu, Joseph M. "Summary and Concluding Remarks." In: *Environmental Tobacco Smoke.* Proceedings of the International Symposium at McGill University. 1989. Lexington: Lexington Books, 1990: 367-375.

(Photo: Greenpeace.)